OUTPUT AND EMPLOYMENT
IN THE IRISH FOOD INDUSTRY TO 1990

*Copies of this paper may be obtained from The Economic and Social Research Institute
(Limited Company No. 18269). Registered Office: 4 Burlington Road, Dublin 4.*

Price £3.00

(*Special rate for Students* £1.50)

A. D. O'Rourke is an Associate Professor in the Agricultural Economic Department of Washington State University, USA and T. P. McStay is a Research Officer of the Agricultural Economics Department, Rural Economy Division, An Foras Talúntais. The Paper has been accepted for publication by the Institute which is not responsible for either the content or the views expressed therein.

OUTPUT AND EMPLOYMENT
IN THE IRISH FOOD INDUSTRY TO 1990

A. D. O'ROURKE and T. P. McSTAY

©THE ECONOMIC AND SOCIAL RESEARCH INSTITUTE
DUBLIN, 1979

ISBN 0 7070 0020 3

CONTENTS

FIGURES

Acknowledgements

The authors are grateful to a large number of people for practical assistance in bringing this study to its completed form. Within both the ESRI and AFT our colleagues were generous and helpful in their comments on the various drafts of the study. We thank them, and also those in the Department of Agriculture and in both the public and private sectors for the advice which was offered as the study developed. Worthy of special thanks are T. J. Baker, E. Attwood and John McCarrick. We are extremely grateful also to Bernadette Payne and Mary McElhone whose assistance in the preparation of the manuscript was invaluable. Finally, we wish to thank all those in the ESRI involved in typing the manuscript at various stages.

General Summary

In 1976 and 1977, the authors undertook an ambitious project to determine likely output and employment in the Irish food industry to 1990, given the continuation of foreseeable trends and relationships. This report documents the major avenues explored in that research and attempts to integrate the findings from the separate sections into a "most likely" scenario for development of the Irish food industry.

In planning this project, we attempted to avoid the pitfalls which have beset so many of the recent studies of the potential for growth in Irish agriculture and the Irish food industry. Some have been partial in emphasis – for example, emphasising production potential and ignoring market potential. Others have lacked adequate documentation for their usually optimistic projections. Others have been exhortations to produce more, rather than cold-blooded assessments of how much more can be produced. And, in general, none have attempted to take into account the dynamic interactions between decision makers and markets which will eventually shape the form of the Irish food industry in 1990. Inevitably, of course, limitations of time, data and expertise have made this report less complete than we would wish. For example, it has not been possible to deal with all supply and service industries. In the years ahead, it is our hope that others will probe in greater depth some of the major questions we have raised but not answered, and that as more data become available, it will be possible to subject to computerised evaluation some of the major interrelationships which we have had to treat fairly subjectively.

Accordingly, in this report we have attempted to discuss the interrelationships of all the major factors likely to affect the future Irish food industry in production, marketing, processing, organisation and policy making. Where possible, we have attempted to quantify the impact of each factor separately and in combination with other factors. Where quantification was not possible, we have attempted to set out in detail the reasons for the judgements made. We do not suggest that this report can give a definitive or final indication of the exact stage of development of the Irish food industry by 1990. However, we do hope that it will provide a basis for broad, objective reassessments of the future place of the food industry in the Irish economy.

Our analysis of the productive potential of Irish agriculture using all available objective criteria suggests that output volume can grow at a maximum of about 2.2 – 2.5 per cent each year, or 38.8 – 45.6 per cent in total between 1975 and 1990. The main limitations to output growth appear to arise not from the inadequacy of Irish farmers (although various deficiencies are noted), but from deficiencies of natural resources (soil, climate, fragmentation of holdings, etc.), and lack of economic incentives to adopt more costly output-increasing technologies.

However, even though our output growth projections are low relative to those of most other commentators, we find that at 1975 price levels, total demand, both export and domestic, is likely to grow less rapidly than output. Most of Irish agricultural output is now sold within the European Community. In the next fifteen years, the combination of slower income and population growth and small response to income growth will mean that demand for food products is likely to grow at a slower rate than in the 1960–75 period. Ireland will perhaps be the one exception to this if emigration remains at a low level, since its birth rates remain high by European standards. Accordingly, expanding sales in the home market, and warding off competition from EC partners may well become the top priority for the Irish food industry in the next decade.

Sales expansion will be difficult if the European Community persists in an agricultural policy which keeps price above competitive equilibrium (so that large surpluses build up) and retains many less efficient producers in agriculture. We argue that a lowering of the real price of food would, in the long run, be most beneficial to Irish agriculture. Many of the part-time or marginal producers throughout the Community would shift to non-agricultural activities. Those farmers in Ireland who have a comparative advantage in farming would then be able to expand production, tap economies of scale, increase their market share of other EC markets and tap market opportunities in third countries. The food processing sector would benefit from an expansion in supplies of raw materials at a lower price and would, in turn, be able to expand markets for its finished products.

The food processing sector itself faces inbuilt constraints on its expansion. Much of the domestic market is served by small native firms or firms which are subsidiaries of foreign multinationals which export on only a limited scale. In those industries most geared to exports, beef and dairy products, the amount of value added, and thereby the employment content, is quite low. Increasing value added would involve development of higher value products and a head-on marketing battle with strongly entrenched multinational food companies which have become dominant in the processing, distribution and sale of higher value added products throughout Europe. Efforts to date by Irish entities, either private or State sponsored, to promote higher value products abroad have met with mixed success.

If present trends continue, by 1990 the Irish food processing industry could be predominantly in the hands of multinational concerns and could be producing about twice its 1973 output with less than 18 per cent more employees. These trends can only be altered by a massive, co-ordinated effort of the major factors in the beef and dairy industry, or by large direct intervention by the Irish Government. However, the risks involved in such intervention would be very great and would have to be offset by clear employment or income benefits that might accrue to the Irish economy. On the one hand, the Irish Government might encourage the creation of Irish-based corporate giants which could compete with existing multinationals, or, alternatively, it might resign itself to the inevitable dominance of multinationals and use tax or other incentives to encourage them to expand their production and exports from Irish plants.

Overall, the Irish food industry can continue to make an important contribution to national income, employment and exports in the 1975–90 period. However, employment growth will be less than one per cent per year, and will only partially compensate for the likely continuing exodus of farmers and farmworkers from agriculture. Accordingly, most of the additional jobs needed in the Irish economy will have to come from the non-agricultural sector.

While we have highlighted certain very serious constraints on the growth of the Irish food industry; limited natural resources, surplus conditions in EC markets, declining response of food demand to income growth, small size and limited organisational strength in the processing sector, etc., there are many steps which could be taken to lessen the burden of those constraints. If reason is allowed to prevail, the Irish food industry can look forward to a healthy future.

Chapter 1

Introduction

SINCE the foundation of the State in 1922, successive Irish Governments have attempted to expand output and employment in order to satisfy the aspirations of all their citizens wishing to live and work in Ireland. While output has risen steadily, employment began to fall at the end of the Second World War, as the decline in the number of people engaged in farming was not offset by the increase in non-farm jobs in Ireland. Rising output and a stable population has meant that the *per capita* incomes of those who remained rose markedly. In the period 1947–68, employment fell by 0.69 per cent per annum, while GNP per employed person rose by 3.40 per cent (Kennedy, 1971, p. 2). The fall in employment was accompanied by high levels of emigration, and until 1961, a fall in the total population. In the 1968–75 period, emigration declined, employment stabilised and GNP per employed person rose at about the same rate as in the earlier period.

The First and Second Programmes for Economic Expansion, 1958–63 and 1963–70, which involved large increases in Government expenditure on economic activities, and coincided with favourable world economic conditions, helped to stabilise total employment, reduce emigration and end the population decline. More significantly for future population and employment trends, the number of persons in the marriageable age-groups, 15–34, began to increase for the first time since the founding of the State. Increased marriages and births, a constant labour force and the gradual drying up of emigration by 1975, led to widespread concern about an unemployment explosion in the years ahead. In a study commissioned by the National Economic and Social Council, Walsh (1975) suggested that in order to ensure full employment by 1986, the number of additional new jobs required during 1971 to 1986 could be in the range 300,000 to 340,000. Between 1971 and 1975, there was an actual decline of 13,000 in total employment. Accordingly, the number of new jobs required annually for the next decade by Walsh's projections is at least 30,000. Furthermore, the successful provision of so many new jobs would stimulate a level of economic growth which could generate further population increases and new job requirements in the years 1986–2000.

Clearly, it is of paramount importance for the Irish to find out as quickly as possible if none, some, or all of the target of 30,000 additional jobs annually can be achieved. If all of the target can be achieved, a resumption of emigration and further rises in unemployment can be avoided, but the nation will need to know what the costs will

13

be in terms of new investment, worker training, acquisition of managerial skills, etc. The less close to the target we can come, the greater will be the impact on Irish society of emigration and/or unemployment. The availability of an additional 30,000 young, educated workers each year can also be viewed as an economic asset and an economic opportunity. Full utilisation of that asset depends on the ability of entrepreneurs to wed labour with the necessary managerial leadership, organisation, capital and market access. In the past, entrepreneurs in the United Kingdom or the United States have been able to exploit the economic opportunities offered by surplus Irish labour. The key question for policy makers is whether that asset can or should be employed in Ireland for the benefit of the Irish nation, and how it might be done.

Government employment policies in the past have tended to focus on two sectors, agriculture and manufacturing industry, on the assumption that employment in the very large services sector would be stimulated by prosperity in the other two sectors. Most of the efforts to aid agriculture have been aimed at the farmer and at production of a greater output or greater farm value of raw agricultural products for the UK market. However, after the Second World War, the UK policy of subsidising expansion of domestic output while purchasing imported food at lower prices, speeded up the loss of jobs in Irish agriculture. Over the 50-year period since 1926, Irish agriculture lost 8,000 workers annually. Employment growth in manufacturing industry compensated for less than one-third of that decline.

Government has tried two broad approaches to job creation in manufacturing (a) protecting the domestic market for Irish industry, as in the 1930s, and (b) reduction of barriers and extension of incentives to foreign investors to set up industries selling to export markets, as in the 1960s. While protection contributed to the growth and consolidation of many Irish industries, it was easily applicable to only a limited number of industrial activities where native raw materials were available or the scale of enterprise was suitable for the small domestic market. In addition, it was incompatible with the post-war efforts by GATT to reduce barriers to trade between nations, and the apparent success of enlarged free trade areas such as the EEC and EFTA.

During the 'sixties and early 'seventies, many foreign investors set up successful manufacturing operations in Ireland. Indeed, the Third Programme for Economic and Social Development 1969–72, published in 1969, mentioned concern that "the growth of foreign-promoted industry may lead to an industrial structure controlled substantially from outside the country". The obvious alternative of promoting Irish-owned manufacturing operations as a basis for increased employment was not particularly successful. The success of the Industrial Development Authority (IDA), in providing new jobs was totally offset by the loss of existing jobs in the older industrial sectors, in spite of the efforts of such bodies as Foir Teoranta to support firms in difficulties. Irish manufacturing imported much of its raw materials and capital equipment and relied on export markets to absorb any increases in output. It was hurt by a number of factors including world-wide recession and rising costs of inputs.

Many commentators argued that emphasis in manufacturing should again be placed on Irish-owned companies using Irish natural resources for their raw materials. While there appeared to be long-term potential for employment increases in exploitation of Irish mines, fisheries and onshore and offshore oil and gas, the most immediate prospects were thought to be in the Irish food industry based on livestock and crops.

The Irish Food Industry

This study, then, is essentially concerned with output and employment potential in the Irish food industry. It covers primarily those manufacturing industries listed in Table 1.1. The first six industries listed depend almost entirely on raw materials from Irish farms. The remaining industries depend in varying degrees on domestic raw materials. However, some of the remaining industries are important as the sole or dominant market for certain farm products, for example, the malting industry for malting barley. Milling is included, although over half its output must be fed to animals before becoming food. The poultry industry, which is not covered by the Census of Industrial Production, is not included, nor are those food firms too small to be included in the Census of Production.

Clearly, in terms either of employment or net output, the food and drink industry is a major contributor to total manufacturing. Both employment and net output have grown over the last twenty years, despite declines in some of the component industries, notably baking, distilling and malting. In many rural areas where a male is the sole earner in a household, the high proportion of males employed in most food industries has important effects on social structure.

The choice of 1990 as a target year for exploration of potential expansion of employment and output was to some extent arbitrary. However, there was a need to choose a target year sufficiently close that realistic economic projections could be made from existing data, and yet sufficiently far ahead to allow Government, trade organisations and private firms the time to make the necessary adjustments to achieve that potential. Indeed, an important objective of this study is an exploration of the steps needed to go from the 1977 level of employment and output to the 1990 potential.

The essential procedures involved in a study of this kind are fairly simple. The demand for the services of a food industry are derived from the amount and form of food demanded by consumers. The food industry's ability to meet that demand depends on its ability to acquire the necessary raw materials; capital and labour and skill in product transformation, and to supply the finished product to the market at a profit. In practice, the profitable matching of supply with demand is dependent on many economic, social, political, technological and other factors, which vary from product to product and between farmer, processor, distributor and consumer.

Accordingly, the data needed to project the potential of the Irish food industry have, of necessity, been drawn from many different sources in many different disciplines. The authors have encountered both major data gaps and a plethora of conflicting data on crucial issues, as well as every combination between these extremes. However, a report such as this would not have been possible without the benefit of

Table 1.1: *Net output and employment of leading sectors of the Irish food and drink industry, selected years, 1953–1973*

	Industry	Short title	Net Output (£ thousand)			Employment (thousands)		
			1953	1963	1973	1953	1963	1973
1.	Bacon factories	Bacon	2885	4250	16189	3.6	4.4	4.6
2.	Meat factories (other than bacon)	Meat	1105	3775	19373	1.3	2.7	4.2
3.	Creamery butter, cheese and other edible milk products	Dairy	3751	5056	33874	4.3	4.8	8.3
4.	Jams, jellies, preserves, canned fruits and vegetables	Canning	1577	2796	9030	2.3	3.4	3.3
5.	Grain, milling and animal feeding stuffs	Milling	3558	5843	19691	4.9	5.1	4.7
6.	Manufacture and refining of sugar	Sugar	1876	2798	7966	a.	2.7	1.9
7.	Manufacture of cocoa chocolate and sugar confectionery	Confectionery	5379	4424	11370	7.7	5.1	5.1
8.	Bread, biscuit and flour confectionery	Baking	5993	8781	23550	10.7	9.6	9.5
9.	Margarine, compound cooking fats and butter blending	Margarine	478	795	2305	0.4	0.3	0.4
10.	Miscellaneous food preparations (including fish)	Miscellaneous	225	596	4513	0.2	0.9	1.7
11.	Distilling	Distilling	602	932	2094	0.9	0.7	0.4
12.	Malting	Malting	540	873	2298	0.8	0.8	0.4
13.	Brewing	Brewing	6994	13180	40504	4.6	4.7	4.5
14.	Aerated and mineral waters	Soft drink	1031	2056	11627	1.6	1.6	2.1
15.	Total Food (Rows 1–10)	Food	26747	39114	147861	35.4	39.0	43.7
16.	Total Drink (Rows 11–14)	Drink	9167	17041	56523	7.9	7.8	7.4
17.	Total Food and Drink		35914	56155	204384	43.4	46.8	51.1
18.	Total manufacturing		81502	173548	696084	142.9	168.2	203.3

a. Included with confectionery.

Source: Net output: *Irish Statistical Bulletin: Quarterly Industrial Production Inquiry* (quarterly). Employment: *The Trend of Employment and Unemployment* (annual).

work done by many scientists, both in Ireland and abroad, in throwing light on the issues encountered in this study.

The report falls into four sections:

(1) an analysis of the sources of growth of agricultural output in Ireland and a projection of the maximum growth attainable by 1990.

(2) an analysis of the major markets in which that agricultural produce can be sold and a projection of the sales volume attainable by 1990.

(3) projection of the value of gross and net output and employment attainable by the Irish food and drink industry in 1990 if projected supply and demand is forthcoming.

(4) summary of the implications of the supply, demand and processing projections for the national and regional economies and for the future plans and policies of leaders in agriculture, industry and Government.

This report differs from previous studies both in its global approach, and in its attempt to project what the interaction of supply, demand and institutional factors portend for the Irish food processing industry.

Chapter 2

General Principles of Integrated Development

I N analysing potential development in the Irish food industry it is important to keep in mind the interrelatedness of economic activities. The development proposed must be able to survive on its own volition in the international, national and local economic and social order likely to prevail in the 1990s. There is a real temptation for projections more than a decade in advance to be "pie-in-the-sky" in nature. For example, using technical coefficients one could argue that by increasing fertiliser usage, Irish grassland *could* by 1990 support 20, 40, or 60 per cent more livestock than at present – therefore, the output of Irish meat factories *should* increase by 20, 40, or 60 per cent. But most Irish farmers will only use additional fertiliser if economic rewards are sufficient to offset the added cost. Some, because of age, lack of initiative or other reasons may prefer to remain at their existing level of operations. The economic rewards will depend both on the price of cattle (probably set within the EEC agricultural system) and on the price of fertiliser, prices for oil and natural gas and other raw materials. Without belabouring the point, technical feasibility alone is not enough to ensure development. Integrated development requires a harmonious combination of all the factors relevant to a successful operation.

Events in recent years have emphasised the impact of the changing world political and economic scene on Irish agriculture. For example, the growth of Irish food production will be affected by whether the world in 1990 is in a state of chronic food shortage or of food surplus. Strengthening of economic ties between East and West may bring larger potential markets or greater competition for our traditional markets. The North-South dialogue between developed and developing countries may bring weakened protection in those agricultural products, for example, sugar, where developing countries have a comparative advantage.

The Anglo-Irish Free Trade Agreement and accession to the European Economic Community have altered fundamentally the opportunities available to the Irish Government for independent economic policies. Ireland, North and South, has increasingly become an economic unit for production and trade in agricultural products. By 1990, if present plans mature, few barriers to trade in agricultural products between Ireland, the UK and EEC member countries will remain. Irish lamb will sell freely in France, Danish bacon will sell freely in Ireland. With free movement of capital and labour within the EEC, the only reason for Irish people to get their food supplies from Irish sources will be if the Irish food industry can compete with its European rivals. Veterinary restrictions, which at present provide protection against imports of certain meat and dairy products, will come under increasing attack from Community partners.

For the Irish food industry to expand, it must be able to acquire simultaneously the needed raw materials, skilled labour, management, capital, technology, supporting services, market access and organisation. It will have to be able to compete with other employers for that labour, management and capital. Without adequate supporting services, notably storage and transportation, it will be unable to supply its customers adequately. Unless its organisations are geared to those of the markets it serves, it will be hampered in its selling activities.

This is not to suggest that there is one single development path which, if entered on now, will lead automatically to the maximum potential of the Irish food industry by 1990. In any decade, the balance of economic advantage will first favour one approach, then another different approach. For example, within countries and within companies, the processes of centralisation and decentralisation ebb and flow as economic and social conditions change. A strong Irish food industry is likely to be built, not on a single raw product or processing technique or market, but on a flexible and diversified approach. While commitments must be made to specific types of plants and processes, labour skills, etc., it is important to keep options open as new technologies and new markets develop. Therefore, recommendations produced in this study with regard to the future strategic development of the food industry in Ireland should be viewed as specific only in the light of information currently available, and do not eliminate the need to constantly reassess strategy as the development process continues.

A further reason for retaining flexibility is the instability of both the supply and price of agricultural raw materials for the food industry. Crops are subject to variations in both acreage and yield in response to changes in the prices of outputs and inputs, weather, disease, etc. Livestock are subject to strong cyclical influences as farmers build or draw down breeding stock. In addition, in the Irish meat industry, supplies of cattle for slaughter are affected by the buoyancy of demand for live cattle in other countries. Prices tend to be equally unstable. Marginal changes in total world supplies often cause significant changes in the relatively small free world market, which in turn affects protected markets such as the EEC. Such uncertainty makes long-term planning by food processors difficult.

A diversified approach to development is also desirable because of the conflicts between the different goals society may have and between the alternative means which may be used to achieve these goals. Increased size may conflict with increased efficiency, firm efficiency with industry efficiency. Increased output may not be compatible with increased profits. Adding a further stage of processing may cause loss of traditional markets for raw products. The private good of individual firms may conflict with the public good. Benefits to one sector may be costs to another, e.g., subsidisation of agriculture to maintain farm prices may penalise consumers. In the best of worlds, such conflicts would not arise, but in the world as it exists, given our limited knowledge and vision, only some of society's objectives can be satisfied at any one time.

Finally, the process of development itself may be a source of conflict within a society. Development must be at a pace and of a form acceptable to society if it is to retain voluntary support for long. Too often, in economic and political debate, there is an underlying assumption that if one per cent growth is good, two per cent growth is better and three per cent growth is better still. However, economic development in a competitive world cannot take place without simultaneous changes in social attitudes and behaviour and the factors which influence them, e.g., education, transport, communication and political, social and religious institutions. The old way of life (usually defined at some pleasantly distant period in the past) is likely to be transformed by further development. Society must choose how much of the old it is willing to give up for the benefits of added employment, increased incomes, etc., resulting from development.

In general, this paper assumes that Irish society, at this point in time, wants more development rather than less, that it is not yet at a point where the majority want to call a halt to growth because of the cumulative disadvantages. However, where alternative paths of development have different types and levels of disadvantage, we will attempt to point them out.

SECTION I

AGRICULTURAL OUTPUT GROWTH TO 1990

Chapter 3

Ireland's Natural Resources for Agriculture

THE productivity of agriculture is heavily dependent on natural resources such as soil, heat and precipitation. Both the total amount and timing of availability are critical. Man has been able to improve the potential of the resources with which he works, for example, by fertilising poor soil, but still lacks control of other ingredients such as sun and rain. Future productivity will depend both on controllable and non-controllable factors. Consistently high yields can only be assured when the influence of the non-controllable factors (wind, drought, etc.) is either greatly reduced, or can be compensated for in controllable factors. For example, development of seeds which germinate at lower temperatures can reduce the heat requirements in the spring.

A realistic appraisal of Ireland's current natural resources for agriculture is absolutely essential to any realistic projection of future productivity. There are numerous clichés about the richness of Irish soil, the mildness of the Irish climate, its natural advantages for grassland, etc., which need to be put in perspective, if we are to assess the real potential of Irish agriculture.

The Irish climate both helps and hinders different types of farm enterprises. Ireland's location between 51° and 56° North of the Equator, places it near the northern limit for production of many temperature zone crops. The moderating influence of the Gulf Stream reduces the extremes of winter temperatures one might expect at this latitude, but any advantage in length of growing season is offset by untimely cloud-cover or rainfall borne by the westerly prevailing winds. The mild winters have made it possible for cattle to overwinter out of doors, thus permitting poorly capitalised farmers to retain cattle, even though cattle make little or no weight gain. In contrast, as Crotty (1966) points out, the severity of Danish winters forced Danish farmers wishing to expand production to house their cattle and provide the necessary feed during the winter to ensure weight gain and recover feed and housing costs. Thus, the mild winters may have been as much a hindrance as a help to greater output in the cattle industry.

Ireland's average rainfall of about 1 metre (approximately 40 inches) per year is not excessive for agricultural purposes. However, its distribution throughout the year, and its interaction with other factors cause problems for farmers. Rain occurs about 200 days per year, and frequently interferes with planting, cultivating and harvesting of crops and other farm operations. Since drainage on Irish soil is often poor, excess moisture cannot be rapidly dispersed. In conjunction with prevailing temperatures in spring and autumn, airborne evaporation is retarded. In addition, in most of Connacht, Ulster and West Munster, rainfall is substantially above the national average.

The mean duration of bright sunshine has greater seasonal extremes than rainfall, ranging from about one hour per day in January to six hours per day in June. However, even during the main growing season, April-September, the uncertain incidence of cloud cover and rainfall makes sunshine duration equally erratic. For crops such as sugar beet, solar radiation may be the limiting factor in determining yields (Lee and O'Connor, 1976).

Hail, sleet, snow and wind are also impediments to agriculture in certain areas. Wind is particularly a problem in the western half of the country near the Atlantic influences and in the flat central plain. In general, wind has not been harnessed to provide electrical power for farm operations, although this may become more feasible if costs of alternative energy sources rise. Together, the above climatic conditions favour the production of forage crops and cattle over other enterprises on most Irish farms.

In the last two decades, tremendous strides have been made in classifying the soils of Ireland and in relating soil types to agricultural potential. We are still a long way from having a complete guide to the productivity of Irish soils, but much has been done to make evaluation of that potential more precise. Of the total land area of approximately 17 million acres, about 12 million acres is currently used for agricultural purposes, the remainder being woods and plantations, grazed and barren mountain, turf bog, marsh, water, roads, etc. However, the National Soil Survey has estimated that only 43 per cent (or 7.3 million acres) is good land, and a further 1.7 million intermediate in quality, so that almost 3 million acres currently in use for agriculture (one-quarter of the total) would be categorised as marginal.

The chief factors used in differentiating soils have been drainage, composition, and elevation. All the soils in the "good" category are dry mineral lowlands. The "intermediate" category is partly wet mineral lowland. Roughly half of the "marginal" category is mountain and hill and a quarter each low level peat and wet mineral lowland. The problem of marginal soils is complicated by their wide dispersion throughout the country, so that in many cases there is a mixture of soil types even within farms. As a result, the productivity of neighbouring farms is much less homogeneous than would be expected in a small country. Mountain and hill land occurs mostly in the west and south-west, the wet mineral lowland in the north-west and west and the low level peat in the west and midlands. The west, not surprisingly, has the lowest proportion of good land.

A further useful breakdown of Irish soils developed by Gardiner and Ryan (1969) of the National Soil Survey related to various degrees of limitations to agricultural use. Forty-six per cent of Irish agricultural land has slight or moderate limitations to use for agricultural purposes. More than half has moderate to strong, strong or very strong limitations. In terms of use-range, 32 per cent has a wide range of uses and a further nine per cent a somewhat limited range, all the rest having serious limitations on choice of enterprise. All three classifications cited suggest that somewhere between 40 and 50 per cent of Irish land has potential for large and diversified production, but that the remaining land suffers from problems of altitude, soil depth, poor drainage, steep slopes, rock outcrops, etc., which limit the type and volume of output more or less severely. Some effort has been made to relate productivity to soil types. A study by Lee and Diamond (1972) showed that the top one-third of Ireland's land area would support up to three times as many livestock units per acre as the lowest third. In another study, Lee (1975) estimated that the best dry mineral soil could support 60 livestock units on 21.1 hectares (52 acres) while the worst wet mineral soil would require 44.2 hectares (109 acres). The relationship between soil type and output of crops is complicated by the greater sensitivity of tillage to the level and distribution of weather factors. In addition, the yield of tillage crops is affected by other factors such as cultural practices, management, etc., whose effects are difficult to separate from the inherent properties of the soil.

Numerous commentators have noted that the problems of availability and quality of soil in Ireland are magnified by its perverse distribution. Where the land is poorest, farms tend to be smallest and therefore most dense. As Lee notes, "It is estimated that 70 per cent of the 'marginal' land occurs in the eight western seaboard counties." Lee also found that average farm size was positively and significantly related to the percentage of dry (i.e., good) land in a county. Government's response to over-crowding in poor land has been to set a target for farm income either in terms of the acreage of good land needed for a "viable" farm or in terms of comparable levels of non-farm income. In either case, given constant prices of outputs and inputs, the target implied that the number of farms must be reduced if the surviving farms were to become viable. In addition, the target based on relative non-farm income moved upwards more rapidly than did actual farm incomes, so that despite continuous decline in the number of farmers the relative income gap tended to persist. The proportion of holdings of less than 50 acres in 1970 was 69.1 per cent, a decline of only 5 per cent since 1955. By province, the proportion in 1970 was 62.2 per cent in Leinster, 57.0 per cent in Munster, 82.6 per cent in Connacht and 79.8 per cent in Ulster.

Fragmentation of many farms among separate holdings is also a problem. A 50-acre farm will often consist of two or three separate parcels of land some distance apart. Costs of machinery set-up, rotation of grazing, and management, will tend to be greater than on a single unit farm. Differences between the parcels of land in soil type, drainage, water availability, shelter, etc., add to the difficulty of exploiting the full potential of such a farm.

The interaction of farm size and structure effects, managerial and climatic factors, etc., has made measurement of differences in productivity in actual farm situations less clearcut than would appear from controlled experiments. Johnson and Conway

Figure 3.1: *Net product per adjusted acre for farms with good demography and 1-2 labour units, by soil type.*

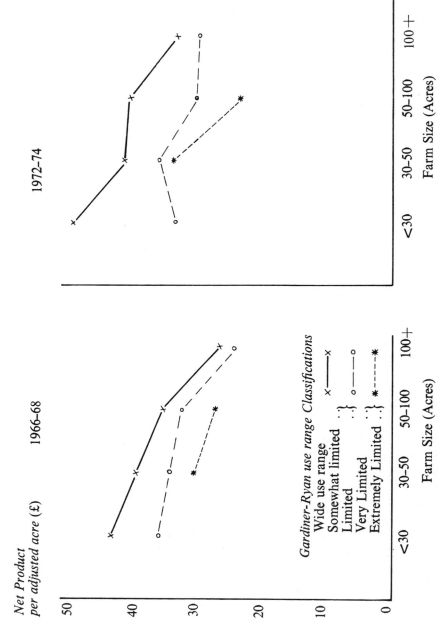

Source: Johnson and Conway.

(1976) examined the combined effects of soil type and farm size for 1966–68 and 1972–74 (Figure 3.1). Their results for farms with good demographic characteristics and a labour force of 1–2 units indicated that net product per adjusted acre tended to be higher for better soils and smaller farms. However, it is worthy of note, that the gap between the best and worst soils in this sub-sample was no wider than the gap between smallest and largest size groups. In fact, one finds the rather remarkable result in both periods that farms of less than 50 acres on the poorest soils had equal or better net product per adjusted acre than farms of over 100 acres on the best soils. Clearly, the manner in which soil is utilised is important, too. Unfortunately, data are not available to show which factors are most important in interacting with soil quality to generate higher net product.

A number of studies have compared the relative performance of selected enterprises in dryland and wetland areas, which correspond to the wide use and limited use categories of Gardiner and Ryan (1969). Hickey (1975) showed that dryland areas had an absolute advantage in net product per acre in all systems of farming studied, but that the comparative advantage was least in drystock systems. Hickey and Connolly (1975) reported similar small differences for single and multiple suckling, bucket rearing and finishing of stores.

Various efforts have been made to increase the productivity of the natural resources used in Irish agriculture. Much recent attention has been devoted to the interaction of structural factors such as age, education, cultural and social patterns on productivity of Irish land. However, these can be more properly discussed in the next section, when we look at labour and managerial resources in Irish agriculture. It is sufficient to point out at this stage the widespread belief that much Irish land is currently held by those who use it poorly both in terms of level of output and rate of growth of output, and that redistribution of holdings into larger units of good land would be expected to lead to increased output and an increased rate of growth. At the same time, it would, at least in the short term, lead to further unemployment among farmers. If such a redistribution did not provide more jobs in agricultural processing and related employment than it eliminated on the farm, it could hinder, not help, in the achievement of national employment goals.

Desire for increased agricultural output has led to much research and experimentation on ways to improve the productive capacity of existing soils. For example, Lee and Diamond (1972) used research data to extrapolate the potential grazing capacity of Irish soils if high rates of nitrogen were applied. They suggested that assuming the present structure of land use, it was technically possible to support 10.3 million livestock units on Irish grazing land, about 70 per cent above the most recent peak level of the cattle cycle in 1973. Using 26 sites representing the major soil types of Ireland for four years, 1967–70, Ryan (1974) found that on average, the highest mean rate of nitrogen used (536 kg/ha) yielded 11.8 tons/ha of dry matter, compared to 7.0 tons/ha for untreated control plots. However, the response to nitrogen was curvilinear, little worthwhile response being obtained from mean N levels in excess of 310 kg/ha. A complementary study of the benefits of phosphorus application by Ryan and Finn (1976) showed an increase from 7.7 tons/ha of dry matter on untreated plots to 9.8 tons/ha on plots treated with 23 kg/ha of phosphorus. Little extra yield was obtained from using higher levels of phosphorus. In addition, some soil types showed no significant response to phosphorus treatment. Similar mixed rates of response to potassium were reported by Blagden and Ryan (1972).

The Committee on the Review of State Expenditure in Relation to Agriculture reported in 1970, p. 53 – "There is substantial evidence to show that, while the application of fertilisers to cash crops has been close to, and even above, the optimum, the use on grassland is a long way below the optimum. As grassland occupies over 80 per cent of the total agricultural area of Ireland, this relatively low level of grassland fertilisation has serious implications for the productivity of agriculture as a whole." However, the Committee went on to point out that increased levels of fertiliser use on grassland was intricately linked with more intensive systems of grazing livestock production. The adoption of such systems involves issues of capital availability, managerial skills, profitability, risk aversion and other factors independent of land quality. Some of these issues will be discussed in the following chapters.

While fertiliser use appears to offer the easiest route to increasing output or net product per acre, individual farmers and the farm industry in aggregate have benefited, and can continue to benefit further, from other less dramatic improvements in natural resources. For example, by the end of December 1974, 2.3 million acres had been improved under the Land Project. While some land may have received duplicate grants under different owners at different times, it is clear that much marginal land did not receive any improvement aid under the Land Project. Given the extent of wetlands and their current lower productivity, existing and improved methods of drainage could be applied more widely. Ironically, many farms also lack adequate water supplies either for stock or for supplementary irrigation. The former factor has an important impact on the milk yield of cows while the latter factor can assure high yield of tillage crops even in periods of drought. Of course, the existence of potential yield increases would not alone justify the capital expense involved in increasing water supplies.

The improvements discussed so far all involve capital expenditure either by individual farmers or by Government, where a known additional cost must be weighed against an uncertain, long-term flow of returns. A number of other methods have been shown to increase the productivity of natural resources without necessarily involving new capital costs, for example, more careful selection of animals for breeding, choice of seeds most appropriate for specific soil and climatic conditions, improved rotational systems, improved timing and frequency of fertilisation, mowing, harvesting, etc. It is probable that these techniques can be most beneficially applied when management skill and access to advisory information is above average.

Two further points need to be made about the role of natural resources in increasing agricultural output. The modernisation of agriculture in many other countries has involved the substitution of other inputs for land. This is particularly true in the case of fertilisers for tillage crops, glass-house production of horticultural products and factory-type production of cattle in feedlots, and of pigs, broilers and eggs. So, while the availability of good land may, in our present system, be a constraint on output, this is neither essential nor inevitable in the future. On the other hand, there is a growing appetite of industry, housing, tourism, roads, sewage systems, etc., for land to meet the needs of a growing population. For example, in the decade, 1966–75 inclusive, 173,185 new houses were built in Ireland. Assuming an average density of six houses per acre gives a land requirement of almost 30,000 acres. Much of this will have been land currently in agricultural use, including some prime agricultural land. At the rate of house-building prevailing in the 1972–75 period, new houses alone would absorb a further 60,000 acres by the end of 1990. Of course, each group of new houses requires a complementary supply of roads, schools, stores and other amenities. If land continues to be a major constraint on agricultural output, it will become important, wherever possible, to use zoning to encourage non-agricultural development on land with least value in agricultural production.

Our review of Ireland's natural resources for agricultural production, then, suggests the existence of many serious constraints on growth, some inherent in the soil and climate, others related to the use to which land is put.

Chapter 4

Labour and Management

MUCH of the blame for the low levels of output and income in Irish agriculture in the past has been laid on the persons engaged in agriculture. Many official and unofficial reports have commented on the high average age of the farm population, the low incidence and lateness of marriage, the high dependency ratio, the high rate of emigration, the conservatism and resistance to change, etc. The *raison d'être* of the Agricultural Advisory Service, of much agricultural research, agricultural education and apprenticeship schemes, has been to improve the level of skill of labour and management in Irish farming.

A review of the 1971 Census of Population, the most recent data available, might suggest that the calibre of labour and management in Irish agriculture remains a barrier to improved output and incomes. However, we will argue subsequently, that the Irish farm population may at last be approaching a more adequate composition both in terms of numbers and of quality for future competitiveness.

Labour and management are still usually inseparable on Irish farms. In 1971, of 276,502 persons in the main agricultural occupations, about two-thirds were farmers and a further 20 per cent sons, daughters or relatives of farmers. Just over 1,000 persons were classified as farm managers. Only 12.9 per cent were agricultural labourers, and less than two per cent were market gardeners, nurserymen or other agricultural workers. Thus, two-thirds of all persons in agriculture were involved in management, and more than half the remaining labour force were relatives of the farmer. The ratio of farmers to other farm workers was about two to one, indicating that on at least half of all farms, the farmer was the sole full-time worker.

About 10 per cent of all farmers were females, mostly widowed or unmarried, and (one might argue) involuntary farmers, not career farmers. Of the male farmers, over 20 per cent were 65 years of age or over, and one-third were unmarried. In terms of educational achievement, farmers were below the national average. Only 14.0 per cent of farmers in 1966 had any post-primary schooling, compared to 36.6 per cent for the population at large. Farmers were also limited in the resources available to them. Over one-third had holdings of less than 30 acres. In view of the incidence of poor land discussed in the previous section, it is probable that at least half had holdings of 30 acres or less of equivalent good land.

A comparison of the results of the 1971 and 1961 Census of Population showed a continuation of the century-old decline in the Irish agricultural labour force. However, while the total farm labour force fell by 28.6 per cent the decline for farmers was only 13.6 per cent, whereas the decline for farmers' sons and daughters and other relatives assisting on the farm was 51.0 per cent. Clearly some of the sons and other relatives would return to the farm after availing of wider educational opportunities. However, both the availability of successors on farms and the labour-management ratio fell in the period. The number of agricultural labourers fell by 40.3 per cent, and the number of market gardeners, nurserymen, and other agricultural workers declined by almost one-third.

Some of these changes were magnified in different provinces. In 1971, while Leinster accounted for 23–25 per cent of all farmers and farmers' sons, daughters or relatives, it accounted for 45 per cent of agricultural labourers, 50 per cent of other agricultural workers, 58 per cent of farm managers and over 68 per cent of market gardeners and nurserymen. Munster had roughly the same proportion of farmers and other agricultural workers, while Connacht and Ulster had a much higher proportion of farmers than of other agricultural workers. As one might expect, farmers' sons, daughters and other relatives were relatively more strongly represented on farms over 50 acres. Clearly, farms in Munster and Leinster are better placed in terms of current size, manpower and specialisation, and in terms of prospective experienced successors than the smaller, one-man farms in Connacht and Ulster.

In the last decade, much greater effort has been devoted to specifying the demographic problems of Irish agriculture more precisely, and in particular, to analysing more qualitative elements than were covered in previous commissions and censuses. In a study of the low farm income problem in agriculture in the West of Ireland, Scully (1971) looked at the interrelationships between factors such as land tenure, demography, farming systems and level of living. He found the familiar problems of aged farmers, small size of holdings, poor education, and low level of living. In addition, he pointed out the absence of clear title to land on over one-third of farms, which made borrowing difficult, the lack of prospective heirs on holdings with older farmers, the absence of intensive farm enterprises, and the lack of off-farm employment. Scully concluded that "All facets contribute, separately or in combination, to the maintenance of the status quo in Western farming. Consequently, any development programme, geared to cater for the farming needs of the Region, should be designed to overcome the restraints embodied in each of them." For the long term, Scully recommended major structural reform so that the land could be worked in viable holdings by the best farmers. In particular, he favoured the return of long-term tenancies as the cheapest way to transfer land from those too old or unable to work it to the young and enterprising.

Hannan (1972) studied the dynamics of social change in the West of Ireland. In contrast to Scully, he showed that very fundamental changes in rural social organisation had taken place and were likely to continue. In particular, he showed that western farmers had become more closely integrated into the national market and social system. This in turn was the source of further change. "Once farm production is linked through the market to family consumption, and family consumption standards are linked directly to the constantly rising aspirations of the urban middle class, a very powerful impetus for change has been introduced."

In all likelihood, the urbanisation of farmer goals began earlier and has progressed faster in the larger and richer farms of Leinster and Munster. For example, in Scully's 1967 sample, while 75 per cent of farm homes had electricity, less than one-quarter had toilets, bathrooms and television sets. Only one-seventh had tractors, one-seventh of dairy herds milking machines. However, in a stratified random sample of Irish farms in 1972, Frawley et al. (1975) found considerably higher levels of amenities and appliances, and classified their sample into four categories, high income, middle income, low income and part-time farmers. High income farmers tended to be younger and better educated, to have the highest incidence of amenities and appliances and to enjoy more holidays and travel abroad. Part-time farmers (who usually have a non-farm job) generally were ahead of middle-income farmers in all categories. The 1973 Household Budget Survey showed similar levels of ownership among farm families as those reported by Frawley et al. However, some gaps between farm and urban levels of living remained. All farm households had a level of electricity availability and car ownership close to that of urban households, but less than half the rate of telephone ownership and two-thirds the ownership of washing machines, refrigerators and rented television sets.

Frawley et al. (1975), in two significant papers attempted to identify successful farm managers by their personal characteristics, attitudes and behaviour. Although interpretation of results proved difficult, Frawley et al. (1975) reckoned that while personal and social factors were not as important as farm factors (e.g., acreage farmed, soil, etc.), they had a significant effect on farm performance. "In order of importance [they suggest] the characteristic which is of greatest value in identifying successful farm managers is the level of living index of the farm family. Next in rank is the previous work experience of the farmer while the level of formal education is the third most revealing factor." The finding that family consumption standards are linked to farm performance coincides with the theory outlined by Hannan (1972). However, it should be pointed out that the analysis carried out by Frawley et al. could not separate which was cause and which effect.

In a second paper, they showed that large farmers (over 120 good acres) differed significantly from small farmers (less than 40 good acres) most notably in being seven years younger on average, having a longer planning horizon and being three times as likely to be involved in farm organisations. Small farmers, on the other hand, were three times more likely to be part-time operators. The response of farm performance to changes in education, level of living and number of dependents was much greater on large than on small farms.

One negative finding by Frawley et al. is also of relevance. "Although farmer age was found to be significantly associated with farming performance in bivariate analysis, its effect on performance is not significant when other factor effects were taken into account . . . This finding must be of special concern in view of the general emphasis age receives in the formulation of certain agricultural policies." Johnson and Conway (1976) later suggested that the combined effect of age and family situation was more relevant to farm performance.

Johnson and Conway analysed Farm Management Survey data in an attempt to separate further the main factors associated with higher levels and rates of growth of net product on Irish farms. Perhaps their most useful refinement was to point out that good demographic structure of households tended to be associated with higher levels of net product per acre and more rapid growth. Households with good demographic structure analysed were:

Expansion – Households with school or pre-school children and headed by a male.
Transition married – a married couple under age 45 in the household but no children.
Transition unmarried – One or more males under 45 in the household but not married and no children.

Once again, this supports the views of Hannan, and Frawley *et al.* of the influence of farmer's social and personal situation on productivity.

However, farm factors were also important. Johnson and Conway found growth of net product only on farms with over 50 acres on the best soils and over 100 acres on group two soils. Growth arose both from increased livestock numbers and acreage and from increased output per unit, both of which almost certainly involved greater injections of capital. Growth was also concentrated on farms with more than one labour unit, suggesting that such a level of labour input is a necessary complement of increased capitalisation and intensification. In contrast, on smaller farms where increased part-time employment off-farm left less than one labour unit on farms, net product per acre declined and farm operations became less intensive.

In a subsequent paper on the same topic, Conway (1975) suggested that emphasis in agricultural policy needed to be shifted from the concept of the farm as a viable economic unit to that of the farm family as a viable social unit. In his sample, families with poor demography operated over one-third of all farms and 28 per cent of all land. Since families with poor demography also tended to have fewer labour units, poorer soil, smaller acreage and less off-farm employment, this group of farmers would find it difficult to increase their family income and would be a serious deadweight burden in efforts to increase national agricultural output. A critical policy issue for the future is whether these farmers should be allowed to lag or whether Government should put pressure on them to pursue growth in the national interest. Kelleher and O'Hara (1976) make a further distinction between those farmers who could make some changes but are unwilling to do so, and those who are willing and able to make changes but are prevented by structural factors. Where structural factors (e.g., fragmented holdings, lack of water, absence of market outlets or support services, etc.) can be identified, suitable policies can be adopted to overcome them.

However, just how much pressure a democratically elected Government can or should place on citizens reluctant to change involves philosophical and political issues outside the scope of this study.

There is some evidence that under modern conditions, the quality of labour and management on Irish farms has improved. Prior to 1970, farm management studies generally showed that net output per acre declined as acreage increased, presumably due to greater intensity of labour usage on smaller farms. However, Conway's analysis of comparable farm survey data for 1955–57, 1966–68 and 1972–74 showed that by 1972–74, the highest net product per acre in the South, North and West was found on 30–50 acre farms, and in the East and Midlands on 50–100 acre farms. This suggests that expansion of output on Irish farms is now being sought by greater application of modern technology, fertilisers, chemicals, machinery, etc. (rather than labour) per acre. In the past the small Irish farmer could achieve a satisfactory income from a limited acreage by producing a higher net product per acre. As the level of satisfactory income rises, this becomes more difficult.

There is also much evidence that the demographic structure of Irish agriculture is improving due to both natural attrition and what Tolley (1970) describes as the replacement of low-level management. For example, between 1951 and 1971, while the total number of all farmers fell by 23 per cent, the number of female farmers fell by 48 per cent and the number of males aged 65 or over by 34 per cent. At the same time, examination of age cohorts at different censuses shows that net new entrants to the occupation of farmer tended to be mostly in the age-group 25–39. For example, between 1961 and 1971, while male farmers showed a decline of about 28,000, this masked a net outflow of about 66,000 (mostly older males) and a net inflow of about 38,000 (mostly younger males). Most of these new entrants would be farmers' sons or relatives succeeding to the farm. In general, they would be better educated than their fathers. The proportion of farmers under 45 rose in every province between 1961 and 1971. More of these younger farmers were married males, who would be considered as expansion farmers in the Johnson-Conway terminology. Furthermore, while about 60 per cent of persons claiming to be farmers at the 1971 Census of Population had less than 50 acres, the remaining 40 per cent of larger farmers are estimated to have farmed over 70 per cent of the land. That is, over two-thirds of Irish farm land is already in units of 50 acres or more. Given the maintenance of long-term trends, by 1990 even more of Irish agricultural land will be in larger farm units. While we do not know how much of the land held by larger farmers would be classified as good, all available evidence suggests that this land is likely to contribute more than proportionately to total agricultural output. Undoubtedly, serious demographic problems still remain in Irish agriculture, but economic and social forces already underway will bring about notable improvements in the next two decades.

Our review of labour and management on Irish farms leads us to more optimistic conclusions than those of most commentators. Contrary to the common stereotype, the farmer population has changed significantly and will continue to change in the future. While not all the problems of aged or unskilled farmers will be eliminated rapidly, the bulk of good Irish farm land is moving into the hands of efficient and modern farmers.

Chapter 5

Patterns of Output

CLEARLY with any given complement of land, labour and management the output of Irish farms individually and collectively can still vary widely as a result of the pattern of output chosen. Inevitable, too, trade-offs will be involved in any efforts to increase production. For example, Crotty (1966) has argued that tillage and dairying are to some extent complementary but that both are competitive with beef cattle production for scarce land. In addition, the outputs in one form of enterprise are the necessary inputs for another. Conserved hay and silage provide winter feed for cattle. Calves from dairy herds provide replacement stock for both the dairy industry and the beef industry. If an individual farmer wishes to expand his output or income he needs to be concerned primarily with trade-offs on his own farm. He can weigh the benefits of 10 additional acres of feeding barley against the loss of 10 acres of grazing land. However, if the agricultural industry as a whole is to avoid severe price and income and production dislocations, it must ensure that linked enterprises grow in unison. For example, in total it may be difficult to increase beef production permanently without an accompanying increase in the dairy herd. It may be difficult to increase tillage acreage over present levels without reducing beef production.

In this chapter, therefore, we look at past patterns of production on Irish farms, and examine to what extent, under modern conditions, these still act as a constraint on aggregate output. It will not be necessary to review the past in great detail since this has been well documented by Crotty, Attwood, O'Connor, Kearney, Hickey and others, but rather to pick out highlights relevant to future policy.

A comparison of crop acreage, livestock numbers and agricultural output in 1965 and 1975, while subject to the usual cautions about single-year comparisons, indicates the broad directions in which the patterns of Irish agricultural output have changed. The most notable changes in the last decade have been the decline in corn crops by 100,000 acres, the decline in root and green crops by 158,000 acres, and the increase in hay and grass for silage acreage by 600,000 acres almost all in grass for silage on the larger farms (Table 5.1 and Figure 5.1). This reflects a swing away from tillage and towards more intensive stock-raising. The increase in stock-raising has been concentrated in cattle, since sheep, pig and poultry numbers are all below 1965 levels. Acreage of feeding barley has risen by one-third to 439.1 thousand acres over half of all corn crop acreage. Clearly, the growth of the dairying and beef industry in the last decade has been, to some extent, at the expense of crop production not

Figure 5.1: *Acreage Devoted to Selected Crops, 1963–75.*

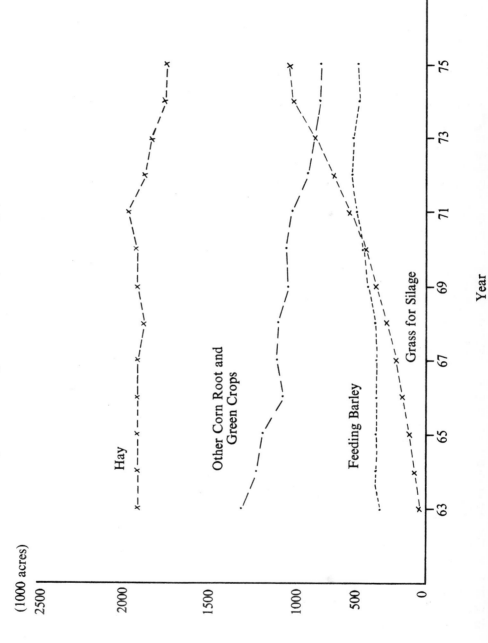

intimately linked to those industries. Of the approximately 900 thousand additional acres devoted to feeding barley, silage and pasture, about 20 per cent was land formerly in hay. Half of the remainder came from other tillage crops and half from increased land under crops and pasture. There is no way of knowing how much of the additional land under crops and pasture results from land improvement and reclamation and how much from changes in definition.

Table 5.1: *Crops and livestock in Ireland, 1st June, 1965 and 1975*

Description	Unit	1965	1975	Changes absolute	Per cent
Corn crops	acres (1000)	939.1	836.4	−102.7	−10.9
Root and green crops	,,	445.0	287.0	−158.0	−35.5
Fruit etc.	,,	10.7	8.8	−1.9	−17.8
Total crops and fruit	,,	1,394.8	1,132.2	−262.6	−18.8
Hay and silage	,,	1,971.4	2,570.5	+599.1	+30.4
Grass for silage	,,	101.7	883.5	+781.8	+668.7
Total crops and hay	,,	3,366.2	3,702.7	+336.5	+10.0
Pasture	,,	8,270.1	8,275.2	+5.1	+0.1
Total crops and pasture	,,	11,636.4	11,977.9	+341.5	+2.9
Cows	(1000)	1,547.4	2,035.0	+487.6	+31.5
Heifers in calf	,,	193.3	215.9	+22.6	+11.7
Bulls	,,	15.0	16.8	+1.8	+12.0
Cattle, three years old and over	,,	220.5	209.3	−11.2	−5.1
2–3 years	,,	808.1	1,106.6	+298.5	+36.9
1–2 years	,,	1,216.2	1,698.2	+482.0	+39.6
Under 1 year	,,	1,358.8	1,645.4	+286.6	+21.1
Total cattle	,,	5,359.3	6,927.3	+1,568.0	+29.3
Sheep for breeding	,,	2,262.5	1,777.3	−485.2	−21.4
Other sheep		2,751.2	2,018.7	−732.5	−26.6
Total sheep		5,013.7	3,796.0	−1,217.7	−24.3
Pigs for breeding		142.8	112.4	−30.4	−21.3
Other pigs		1,123.1	730.6	−392.5	−34.9
Total pigs		1,265.9	843.0	−422.9	−33.4
Total poultry		11,404.9	10,412.4	−992.5	−8.7

Source: Irish Statistical Bulletin (Quarterly), various issues.

Within the cattle sector the only group which showed an absolute decline was cattle three years old and over, reflecting the slow movement towards younger finishing of beef cattle. The proportion of heifers in calf and of cattle under one year was lower (although actual numbers were higher) in 1975 when cattle were on the

Table 5.2: *Estimated output of principal agricultural products in Ireland, 1965 and 1975*

Produce	Unit of Quantity	Estimated quantity			Estimated value £000		
		1965 (Thousand)	1975	Change per cent	1965	1975	Change per cent
Cattle and calves	No.	987	2,361	+139.2	64,078	391,038	+510.3
Sheep and lambs	No.	1,853	1,852	—	12,006	29,964	+149.6
Pigs	No.	1,954	1,534	-21.5	31,189	65,142	+108.9
Ordinary fowl	No.	11,489	21,048	+83.2	3,851	12,185	+216.4
Total Livestock		—	—	—	115,828	511,073	+341.2
Milk (a) fresh sale	1000 gal	133	138	+3.8	16,722	45,842	+174.1
(b) industrial	1000 gal	391	624	+59.6	38,058	190,265	+399.9
Wool	lb.	19,373	14,990	-22.6	2,896	2,863	-1.1
Eggs, Hen	120	6,473	5,659	-12.6	10,518	16,015	+52.3
Total livestock products		—	—	—	71,518	256,682	+258.9
Wheat	metric ton	203	189	-6.9	5,284	12,838	+143.0
Oats	,,	41	28	-31.7	914	1,368	+49.7
Barley	,,	419	677	+61.6	9,685	40,263	+315.7
Sugar beet	ton	746	1,407	+88.6	5,908	24,398	+313.0
Potatoes	,,	466	401	-13.9	10,396	23,699	+128.0
Hay	,,	35	24	-31.4	292	805	+175.7
Total crops	,,	—	—	—	39,986	133,490	+233.8
Total crops, livestock and livestock products (a)		—	—	—	227,332	901,245	+296.4

(a) Excluding value of changes in livestock numbers and value of turf.

Source: Irish Statistical Bulletin (quarterly), various issues.

downward phase of the cycle than in 1965 when the herd was being expanded. The data for sheep mask an actual growth in the size of the mountain flock which did not compensate for a fall of one-third in the large lowland flock (Hickey and Kearney 1976). While both pig and poultry numbers have fallen, large changes in concentration and intensification of production have taken place. Pig output actually reached 2,350 thousand in 1972 before falling gradually to the 1975 level (Table 5.2). However, the ratio of output to breeding herd in 1975, was virtually unchanged from 1965. In contrast, increased broiler production of ordinary fowl enabled annual output in 1975 to be doubled on the basis of a smaller June population.

The estimated quantity of output of cattle and calves in the two years, 1965 and 1975, reflected the retention of animals for herd expansion in the earlier year and the running down of herd numbers in the later year. However, even after allowing for such stock changes, the long-term potential for output of cattle and calves had been increased in the decade by at least a third over 1965 levels. The output of all milk was 45.4 per cent higher in 1975 from an approximately 30 per cent increase in dairy cow numbers, the remaining increase in output arising from higher yields per dairy cow. The industrial market – the processing of butter, cheese, skim milk, etc. – was the dominant outlet for increased milk production. Of the main crop products, only barley and sugar beet showed increases in the volume of output over the decade. Both malting barley and feeding barley shared in the increase.

Because of the effects of inflation, changes in the estimated value of output can be best examined relative to the changes for all categories of crop and livestock products, which more than trebled in value in the decade. Regardless of which price index is used for deflation (consumer, wholesale, agricultural, etc.) it is clear that the real value of output rose substantially. For example, deflation by the consumer price index indicates that the real value of total output in the decade rose by 64.6 per cent. Items whose estimated value rose by less than 140 per cent in current terms between 1965 and 1975 suffered a decline in real value. The largest increases in value were in cattle and calves, milk for industrial uses, and barley and sugar beet. Pigs, wool, hen eggs, oats and potatoes suffered declines in real value. The source of increased value of output for livestock and milk was primarily increases in volume, although real prices rose marginally for cattle, sheep and pigs and milk for fresh sale, and by over 20 per cent for milk for industrial use. Prices of wheat and barley moved marginally upward in real terms.

The national shift towards a more livestock-oriented agriculture was also evident by region (Table 5.3). However, the greater concentration of feeding barley acreage in Leinster is symptomatic of a general tendency for the remaining tillage to be concentrated on the better land. Tillage declines have been most severe in Connacht and Ulster. In contrast, cattle numbers have increased fairly uniformly in all provinces, both for milch cows and for all other cattle. The additional needed acreage of pasture, hay and silage and feeding barley for the larger cattle herds came either from increases in total agricultural land or from land withdrawn from other tillage. However, the

Table 5.3: *Area under selected crops and number of cattle, by province, 1965 and 1973*

Item	Year	Crops (1000 acres)				
		Leinster	Munster	Connacht	Ulster	Total
Feeding barley	1965	130.2	168.1	17.7	12.4	328.4
	1973	239.7	181.9	20.3	23.2	471.2
Other corn crops	1965	316.5	160.2	74.2	59.9	610.7
	1973	247.2	92.1	38.8	25.6	403.6
Root and green crops	1965	186.0	145.8	71.4	41.7	445.0
	1973	143.4	97.8	45.9	24.6	311.6
Hay and silage	1965	591.2	762.4	413.2	204.6	1971.4
	1973	747.4	992.7	508.8	261.8	2510.6
Pasture	1965	2673.8	2931.3	1867.4	797.7	8270.1
	1973	2606.7	2934.7	1914.2	807.2	8262.8
Total crops and pasture	1965	3903.5	4171.4	2444.6	1116.8	11636.4
	1973	3990.2	4308.1	2528.3	1142.7	11969.3
		Cattle (1000 head)				
Milch cows	1965	386.1	761.6	258.6	141.1	1547.4
	1973	533.9	1004.7	363.7	194.0	2096.3
Other cattle	1965	1330.9	1381.2	763.1	336.7	3811.9
	1973	1707.2	1777.8	979.3	409.2	4873.5
Total cattle	1965	1717.0	2142.8	1021.7	477.8	5359.3
	1973	2241.1	2782.5	1343.0	603.2	6969.8

Source: Irish Statistical Bulletin, various issues.

total land committed to livestock-oriented enterprises in 1973 but not in 1965 increased only by 5, 6, 7 and 8 per cent, respectively, in Leinster, Munster, Ulster and Connacht. Clearly, the very large increases in output were due, in a much larger measure, to other factors discussed elsewhere in this paper. For example, Crotty has suggested that the wider adoption of silage-making has loosened the winter feed constraint on the number of cattle that can be retained on Irish farms.

While most Irish farms continue to have mixed patterns of output, there have been noticeable trends towards specialisation in certain segments of the industry. The mixed pattern of production makes definition and measurement of enterprise types difficult. For example, the National Farm Survey of 1955–57 abandoned a classification scheme based on proportion of value of output derived from each enterprise for one based more on physical units of measurement, e.g., number of milch cows. However, a comparison of the relative concentration of output in different enterprises in 1955–57, with figures cited by Hickey from the Farm Management Survey for 1972–73, suggests that smaller farms in general are going out of crop production and into cattle, but that dairying remains a very important small farm operation, especially in Munster. Pigs, a non land-using enterprise, have become more important on small farms (5–15 acres) in Leinster and Ulster. Dairying has become much more prominent in farms of 30–50, 50–100 and 100–200 acres in Leinster and Munster, and on 50–100 acre farms in Ulster. Sheep and wool have gained ground only in Connacht. Crop production has lost most ground in Munster and on the smallest farms, and has become more important only on the very largest farms (200 acres and over) in Leinster.

These broad changes in the relative importance of different enterprises conceal the effects of changes in specialisation which are generally thought to have taken place in crops, dairying, pigs and poultry. For example, in December 1975, the number of dairy cows on holdings with dairy cows averaged about 10 cows per holding. Holdings with 10 or more total cattle, 32.9 per cent of all holdings with dairy cows, accounted for 78.9 per cent of all dairy cows. Similarly, in the case of pigs, the average number per holding was 38.3, but over three-quarters of all pigs were on holdings with more than this average figure.

No similar recent data are available for crops. However, Kearney (1976) reports that a study of a matched sample of farms from the Farm Management Survey suggests that:

(1) Where a particular cereal enterprise was omitted from the farm programme it was typically not replaced by another cereal but by dairying and cattle.

(2) Expansion in cereals was generally accommodated by an increase in effective farm size rather than at the expense of livestock enterprises or through intensification.

(3) On better soils a decline in sheep numbers was usually associated with a decline in tillage and an expansion in dairying and cattle.

(4) There is considerably greater mobility in cereal production than in the case

of dairying or cattle which suggests that to some extent the cereal enterprise is a marginal activity.

(5) Where dairying was discontinued, it usually led to a decline in farming intensity. Similarly, the incorporation of dairying in the farm programme was accompanied by an increase in intensity.

Clearly the patterns of output adopted by Irish farms have changed as the amount and distribution of land, the calibre of management, the availability of new techniques and the market opportunities have changed. While the data permit us to see some of the links between these changes, we are far from being able to designate which are cause and which effect. Many public figures have expressed concern about whether the current pattern of output is optimal for agriculture and the nation either on economic or social grounds. For example, further declines in tillage, coinciding with further increases in livestock numbers would create a need for large increases in imports of feed grains, which would partly offset Balance of Payments gains from increased beef exports. Similarly, the swing to more drystock production on small farms appears to worsen the relative farm income situation of this group. In addition, concentration on a small number of livestock products increases the risks involved in international marketing. In the next section, we look at the economic rationale for current output patterns and at what it indicates for future policy.

Chapter 6

Economic Rationale for Output Patterns

T HE essential argument of this section is that Irish farmers are not, as some have argued, perverse, that they have reacted to the economic forces of the market and of public policy and to their own limited resources in determining their pattern of output, and that economic incentive, not exhortation, will be most effective in bringing about future changes. Selected, but by no means exhaustive, evidence is presented in support of these arguments.

In the last chapter, we saw that Irish agriculture, which was already heavily oriented towards livestock in 1965 had become even more so in the following decade, in many cases to the virtual elimination of tillage. National Farm Survey results for the years 1955–57 indicated that cattle enterprises gave the lowest family farm income in all farm size classes. And twenty years later, the Farm Management Survey showed that the income gap had widened against cattle enterprises. As Hickey comments, "The fact that cattle output increased its share of total gross output considerably seems paradoxical when we consider the low level of returns either per unit of land, labour or capital being generated by systems of farming concentrating on cattle production."

The National Farm Survey and subsequent Farm Management Surveys provide a number of clues to explaining away the apparent paradox. We plotted the three-year average results (1955–57) for four patterns of farming, (a) dairying mixed without cash crops, (b) dairying mixed with cash crops, (c) crops mixed and (d) cattle mixed, in a three-dimensional diagram. We inserted the labour units, acreage units and output for each farming pattern and size class. It appeared that these average observations clustered along at least two quite narrow bands (see Figure 6.1) the mixed cattle and dairying without cash crops being much steeper with respect to the labour axis. From these average relationships, we synthesised total output and output per labour unit and per acre for a combination of (b) and (c), the farms with crops, and for (a) and (d), farms without crops (Figure 6.2).

The crop enterprises yielded £700 per labour unit for approximately the same input of labour and about two-thirds of the land input as the non-crop enterprises. A crop farmer wishing to earn the same income by switching to a non-crop pattern would require 50 per cent more acreage. Conversely, a non-crop farmer presently earning £700 per labour unit, who wished to switch to crop farming with a given acreage would need 30 per cent more labour units but earn only £60 extra per labour unit. In all probability, land quality and non-availability of family labour would have prevented many non-crop farmers switching to crop farming, but clearly the economic reward for making such a change was not great.

A comparison of total productivity for the crop and non-crop systems shows an interesting dichotomy. For the same input of labour, both systems had approximately

47

Figure 6.1: *Approximate relationship of acres farmed, labour units and output for different patterns of farming, National Farm Survey, 1955–57.*

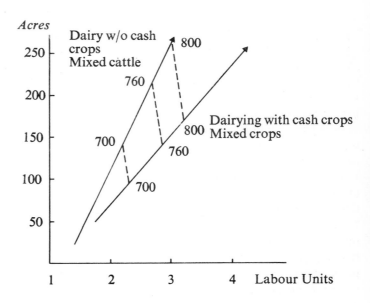

Figure 6.2: *Estimated total output and output per labour unit and per acre for different patterns of farming, National Farm Survey, 1955–57.*

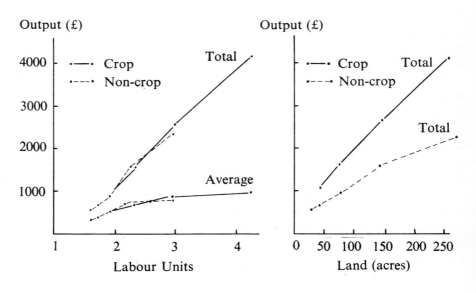

the same total and average output. However, for the same input of land, the crop farms yielded much more total output and average output per acre. The crop farms also appeared to meet diminishing returns less rapidly (although it would obviously be dangerous to make categorical statements based on the limited data). Given the ability of farmers to earn equal returns per unit of labour in crop and non-crop patterns but not per unit of land, one might reasonably suggest that differences in land quality (as discussed in Chapter 3) were a major factor in the differences in output per acre. It is extremely doubtful that farmers are so perverse that they would persist in non-crop enterprises when crop enterprises would yield up to twice as much output per acre unless their land (as is so much Irish land) was relatively unsuitable for production of most crops. The enterprise chosen tended to give the highest return possible with the quantity and quality of land available to each farmer. To some extent, higher returns per unit of labour could be achieved by adjusting the number of labour units to the fixed quantity and quality of land available. In general, that adjustment was to less labour, through out-migration, discussed in Chapter 4. Note, however, that the 1955–57 National Farm Survey gives us only a glimpse at one point in time at the dynamics of enterprise choice. It does not answer some of the questions raised earlier about why a farmer with, say, 150 acres and 2 labour units would be satisfied with a given farm income in 1955 but not in 1975. Clearly, the changing attractiveness of alternative employment and changing income expectations, not just farm resources, would affect decisions whether or not to stay in agriculture.

The Farm Management Surveys of An Foras Talúntais, while differing in sample size, scope, method, and definition from the pioneering National Farm Survey, provide a more recent glimpse of the relationship between different enterprises. The three-year report for the years 1966–69 showed the same relationship of labour and land to output as in 1955–57. Total and average output for a given level of labour input was similar among the main systems of farming. However, the total and average output per unit of land varied widely. Only five systems are shown in Figure 6.3 (for clarity of presentation): hill sheep and cattle, mainly drystock, mainly creamery milk, drystock and tillage, and creamery milk and tillage. The last named gave a similar performance to the liquid milk and creamery milk and pigs systems, which are not separately shown.

Clearly, above 50 acres, the total output increased as one moved from the least intensive to the most intensive systems. Since the return to the same quantity of labour was similar, it is reasonable to conclude that climatic problems, capital limitations, inadequate return on capital or other impediments prevented farmers from shifting readily from their existing to a more profitable pattern of farming. MacCanna's (1976) Report on the World Bank Project, documents the difficulties caused for expansion-minded farmers by capital shortages. An examinstion of how output per acre varied as acres farmed increased shows that mainly drystock and hill sheep and cattle had the traditional shape, declining for farms above 20 acres. However, the systems with tillage showed average output per acre increasing up to well over 50 acres. One might

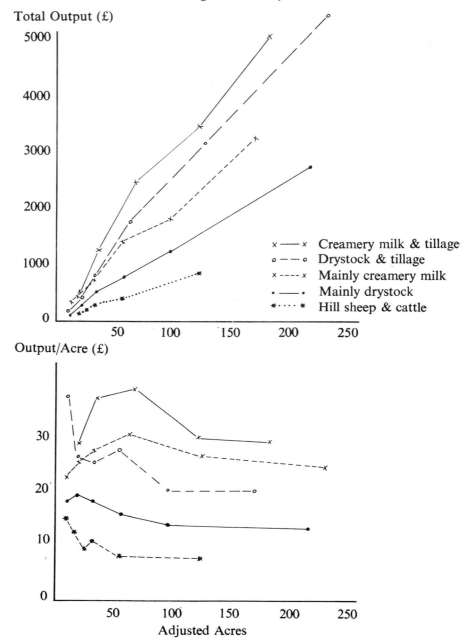

Figure 6.3: *Total and Average Output per acre, by system of farming*, 1966–69, *Farm Management Survey.*

Total Output (£)

x——x Creamery milk & tillage
o – – o Drystock & tillage
x - - - x Mainly creamery milk
•——• Mainly drystock
····· Hill sheep & cattle

Output/Acre (£)

Adjusted Acres

suspect that farms in the 30–100 acre category with tillage have been able to combine most effectively modern seeding, fertilising and other practices with already above average soil. The results for both 1955–57 and 1966–69 suggest that increasing the productivity of the land within existing enterprises may be more effective in increasing aggregate agricultural output, than attempting to switch land to enterprises not now considered suitable by farmers themselves.

A comparison of estimated gross margins per acre in 1965 and 1975, using data reported by Kearney in November 1974 and September 1976 papers, reveals very large changes in the monetary amount but not in the ranking of individual enterprises over the decade (Table 6.1). The increase in real terms was about 60 per cent for wheat, 40 per cent for creamery milk and cattle, less than 30 per cent for other tillage crops (except potatoes, which had a shortage-induced 170 per cent increase) and an actual decline for sheep. Keeping in mind the limited land area highly suitable for wheat, it is clear that the trend to cattle and dairying was economically rational.

Table 6.1: *Estimated gross margins per acre for selected enterprises,*
1965 and 1975

Product	Estimated gross margin		Rank	
	1965	1975	1965	1975
	(£'acre)			
Wheat	21	81	5	3
Malting barley	25	66	3	5
Feeding barley	19	54	6	6
Sugar beet	54	165	1	2
Potatoes	54	350	1	1
Creamery milk	24	80	4	4
Cattle	12	40	8	7
Sheep	15	30	7	8

Source: Kearney, B., op cit.

However, one still is faced by the paradox that gross margins per acre for cattle even at the peak of the price cycle are lower than those for alternative tillage crops. Accordingly, on any given size of farm, family farm income will be lower in cattle than in tillage enterprises. For example, Farm Management Survey results by system of farming for 1975, show that farms with tillage as part of their operations had about five times as much family farm income as mainly drystock farms (Table 6.2). However, tillage farms were almost three times as large and had one-third to one-half more labour per farm. When family farm income is adjusted to a norm of (for convenience) one labour unit and 50 acres, as a measure of comparative return to the same bundle of inputs, the income generated per labour unit and 50 acres among all farms is higher on mainly drystock than on drystock and tillage farms, and the relative disadvantage of hill sheep and cattle farms is greatly reduced. This result occurs because dry stock farms use the minimum of purchased inputs and capital services. In the case of full-time farms (i.e., farms providing employment for the equivalent of at least 0.9 labour units), while the family farm income of mainly drystock farms was higher relative to tillage farms than on all farms, the income per labour unit per 50 acres was lower. However, full-time farms in general tended to have lower output for a comparable bundle of land and labour than all farms. Even on full-time farms, this difference is unlikely to be statistically significant. Apart from the measurement difficulties involved, the variability within categories tends to be great. In addition, similar measures of family farm income per labour unit and 50 acres for different sizes of farm province, and soil type show much greater differences than those arising from system of farming. However, the 1975 pattern shown here is typical of that found for previous years. We conclude that the pattern of Irish farming in the 1970s is not perverse but reflects reasonable economic decisions by individual farmers in light of both the quantity and quality of land available to them and of other limiting factors.

Table 6.2: *Family farm income and income per labour unit per 50 acres farmed*, 1975

Pattern of Farming	Family farm income		Income per labour unit per 50 acres farmed[a]	
	All farms	Full-time farms[b]	All farms	Full-time farms[b]
	£	£	£	£
	(1)	(2)	(3)	(4)
Mainly creamery milk	1786	2165	2069	1804
Creamery milk and tillage	4270	4327	1555	1555
Creamery milk and pigs	3245	3695	2592	2288
Liquid milk	4642	4808	1786	1737
Mainly drystock	876	1398	1809	1085
Drystock and tillage	3238	3677	1511	1366
Hill sheep and cattle	625	927	743	474
All farms	1656	2498	1867	1491

a.   Column (3) was derived from Column (1) by dividing by the average number of family labour units and the average number of 50 acre units (adjusted acres) employed in that pattern of farming. Column (4) was derived from Column (2) in the same way.

b.   Full-time farms. Farms with 0.9 or more of a labour unit working on the farm.

Source: Farm Management Survey, 1972–75 Four-year Report, An Foras Talúntais, Dublin.

This does not imply that the pattern of farming is now optimal or need necessarily be static. We have discussed previously how land quality can be changed by drainage, liming, fertilisation, etc., how low-level management can be replaced by high-level management, and how capital can be substituted for either labour or land, e.g., through use of tractors or through introduction of non-land using enterprises such as pig rearing and fattening. We look next at the economic forces which have induced such changes in Irish agriculture.

Net output of Irish agriculture is defined as gross output (including value of changes in livestock numbers), less cost of purchased farm materials, i.e., feeding stuffs, fertilisers and seeds. Expenses such as rates, repairs, fuel, depreciation, etc., are subtracted and subsidies added to arrive at an estimate of income arising in agriculture. In 1975, income arising was 61.3 per cent and net output 71.1 per cent of gross output. The comparable figures for 1965 were 64.3 and 78.7, and for 1956, 66.4 and 81.6 per cent respectively. In the period 1956–65, each additional £1 of expenditure on purchased farm materials was associated with a £3.6 increase in net output and in the period 1965–75, a £4.2 increase. However, the increase in net output per £1 of total expenses remained at about £2.5 in both periods because of sharp increases in costs of repairs, fuel and depreciation of machinery and implements. That is, there was a greater response to expenditure on farm materials than other expenditures. The rate of response of net output to increased usage of farm materials was less than unity in both periods. A 10 per cent increase in the value of farm materials used generated a six per cent increase in net output in 1956–65 and an eight per cent increase in 1965–75.

These aggregate figures conceal wide divergences in the greater use of purchased inputs by farms of different size, type, location, etc. There is some evidence that a large core of full-time farmers are increasingly sophisticated users of feeding stuffs, fertilisers, etc., and that a further large group of farmers have changed their mode of operation little in twenty years. If economic rationality prevails, one would expect that the first group earned above average absolute and relative returns for increased expenditure on inputs, but that the latter group either were constrained from increased use of inputs, and/or earned unsatisfactory returns from their use. However, there is insufficient evidence to test this hypothesis.

A rough calculation of the changes in relative profitability and use of the main purchased inputs, feedstuffs and fertilisers, support the view that their use by Irish farmers makes economic sense. As a measure of the relative profitability of feedstuffs, we estimated the gross output of livestock products per acre of hay and pasture from 1960–1975, indexed to the base 1960=100, and divided by the wholesale price index for feedstuffs. When output per acre of livestock products was rising faster than feedstuff prices, we would expect it to be relatively more profitable for farmers to purchase additional feed. In fact, use of feedstuffs appeared to follow closely the pattern of relative profitability with some evidence of a one-year lag. In a similar manner, we compared the relative profitability of fertiliser use on tillage

Figure 6.4: *Relationship of relative profitability of feedstuffs and fertilisers to volume used*, 1960–75.

Index (1960=100)

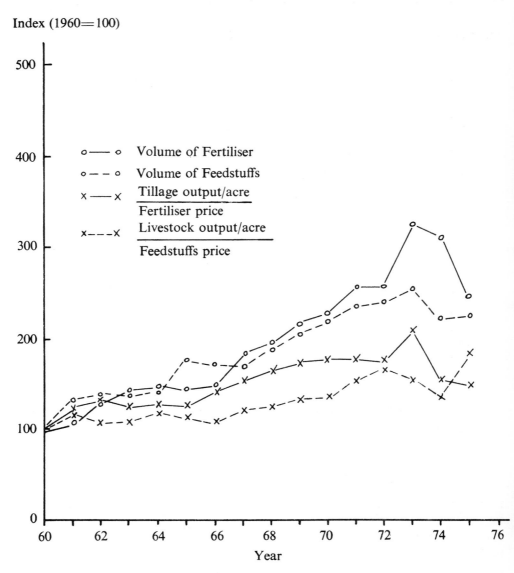

Figure 6.5: *Index of Selected Livestock Product Outputs and Feedstuff Prices*, 1960–75

Index (1960=100)

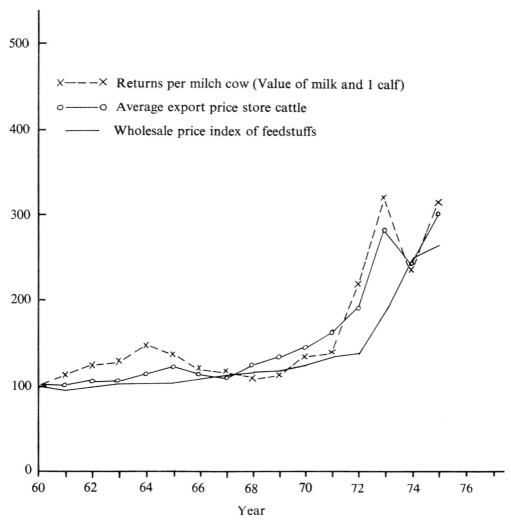

Year

land with the volume of fertiliser used (Figure 6.4). Once again, use and relative profitability were closely linked despite the fact that much fertiliser is also used on grassland. Analysis of fertiliser use studies and yield data suggested that response of yield to increased fertiliser use was always positive but not always strongly so. Of course, Government subsidisation and other factors will have affected the strength of farmers' response to the changed profitability of fertilisers and purchased feeds. These findings are supported by studies by O'Rourke and McStay (1978) which show that the demand for feed and fertiliser has been heavily dependent on the relative prices of farm outputs and farm inputs, both of which are outside the control of the Irish farmer.

For example, Figure 6.5 compares the index of feedstuff price, to base 1960=100, with an index of returns per milch cow and per store cattle exported in the period 1960–75. Returns per milch cow include value of milk output plus the value of one calf. Store cattle price is chosen as most representative of cattle output over the 16-year period. Clearly, dairying could afford more purchased feedstuffs in the years 1960–64 and 1971–73. Purchasing of feedstuffs was increasingly feasible for store cattle in the years 1968–73. However, the experience of 1967 and 1974 in both cattle and dairying indicate the risks of heavy dependence on purchased feedstuffs. The index of value of output of pigs is not shown in Figure 6.5, because it follows closely the pattern of feedstuff prices. That is, for no calendar year in the period 1960–75 has the relative profitability of purchased feedstuffs for pigs improved. Since the pig industry relies so heavily on purchased feeds, this has been an economic disincentive to expansion of pig enterprises. The projections of Josling and Lucey (1972) suggested that under EC CAP conditions, the Irish pig industry would be very vulnerable. This appears to have been borne out in fact.

To summarise this section, we have tried to present evidence that Irish farmers have made rational economic use of the resources available to them in their choice of farming system. Regardless of the farming system chosen, the returns per comparable unit of land and labour (excluding hill farms) have been relatively uniform. Differences in family farm income appear to be due more to the amount of land and labour available than to the pattern of output chosen. Irish farmers also appear to have been rational in their increased use of purchased fertilisers and feedstuffs although the economic incentive has varied in strength from year to year and between enterprises. The trend of both product and input prices will determine the future demand for such inputs.

Chapter 7

Productive Potential of Irish Agriculture, 1990

IN this chapter, we bring together the threads of thought discussed in previous chapters in an attempt to answer a central question of this study, what output can be realised by Irish agriculture in 1990? Of course, many kinds of future are possible. Irish agriculture might revert to cattle ranching, to a dominantly-tillage system, to non-land enterprises such as pigs or poultry or to any one of a myriad possible combinations of different systems. However, not all possible combinations are equally likely. We have shown that the present type and level of output can be rationally explained by the present resources in and the economic incentives for Irish agriculture. Irish agriculture in 1975 has moved in a logical progression from where it was in 1960. One might reasonably expect, then, that many of the economic forces that will affect Irish agriculture for the next fifteen years are already in evidence. Accordingly, we can be hopeful that we can indicate at least the broad direction and likely magnitude of the changes which are realistically possible by 1990.

Land in situ is perhaps the best indicator of the natural resources available to Irish farmers. Land quality is a general term used to indicate the structural and chemical composition of the soil and its ability to interact with sun, rain, wind, snow, etc., to produce crops or pasture. Land quality can be altered by reclamation, drainage and other improvements. The quantity of land of different productivity can be altered by such improvements and by alternative demand for land (Table 7.1). Using as a starting point the 1967 acreage in agricultural and non-agricultural use, and the breakdown of agricultural land by range of use suggested by Gardiner and Ryan (1969), we can then examine how the distribution of land is likely to have changed by 1975 and what this portends for 1990. The assumptions underlying these projections are based on likely patterns during the 1967–75 period. For example, about 100,000 acres of Irish land has qualified for farm improvement grants each year. However, one can only guess at the impact of such improvements. We have assumed that the effect is greater, the better the land initially. Again, we have arbitrarily assumed that half of all improvements on soil classes B and C lead to a re-classification upwards. Our estimate of an additional 200,000 acres requirement of land for roads, houses and other amenities between 1975 and 1990 could, of course, be altered up or down by changes in the rate of population and economic growth.

Despite the tenuousness of some of the assumptions, it is remarkable that the proportion of class A land remains about the same in 1975 and 1990 as in 1967. Non-agricultural land shows a decline of 8.5 per cent between 1967 and 1990. One might question whether that much flood-plain, hill, bog and other improvable land is available. However, the increase in agricultural land shown over the same period, 3.7 per cent, is about half that actually achieved between 1960 and 1975. Since our assumptions lead to an absolute decrease in class B land and an 11.1 per cent increase

57

Table 7.1: *Distribution of Irish land by range of use for agriculture and estimated changes, 1967, 1975 and 1990*

	1967 (1000 acres)	(%) d	Improved 1967-75 a (1000 acres)	Roads, houses etc. b (1000 acres)	Reclassified c (1000 acres)	1975 (1000 acres)	(%)	Improved 1975-90 a (1000 acres)	Roads, houses etc. b (1000 acres)	Reclassified c (1000 acres)	1990 (1000 acres)	(%)
Total land area	17023.7			100.0		17023.7			200.0		17023.7	
Agricultural: of which,	11818.8	100.0	605.1	69.4	+228.5	11977.9			138.8	+422.6	12261.7	
A. Wide or somewhat limited use range	4869.3	41.2	292.2	28.6	+87.5	4928.2	41.1	554.4	57.2	+162.2	5033.2	41.0
B. Limited use range	3498.4	29.6	174.9	20.5	+69.0 −87.5	3459.4	28.9	324.3	41.0	+134.7 −162.2	3390.9	27.7
C. Very or extremely limited use range	3451.1	29.2	138.0	20.3	+228.5 −69.0	3590.3	30.0	269.3	40.6	+422.6 −134.7	3837.6	31.3
Non-agricultural	5204.9		159.1	31.6	+69.4 −228.5	5045.8		283.8	63.2	+138.8 −422.6	4762.0	

Assumptions: a Estimated at 6%, 5% and 4% of 1967 base for classes A, B and C respectively. For non-agricultural is assumed equal to the increase in agricultural land. Estimated in the same manner for 1975-1990.
b Assumed totals allocated among land classes on the basis of total acreage in each land class in the initial year of the period.
c Assumed that all improved non-agricultural land is reclassified as agricultural, class C. Half of all land improved in classes C and B is assumed to move up one class.
d Based on Gardiner and Ryan, 1969.

Sources: Irish Statistical Bulletin, various issues. Gardiner and Ryan.

Table 7.2: *Estimated 1975 and projected 1990 acreage and productivity by class of agricultural land*

Soil class	Area (1000 acres)			Relative productivity			Weighted product		
	1975	1990	% change	1975	1990	% change	1975	1990	% change
A. Wide or somewhat limited use range	4928.2	5033.2	+2.1	100.0	102.0	+2.0	492820	513386	+4.2
B. Limited use range	3459.4	3390.9	-2.0	80.0	81.0	+1.2	276752	274663	-0.8
C. Very or extremely limited use range	3590.3	3837.6	+6.9	70.0	71.0	+1.4	251321	272470	+8.4
Total agricultural land	11977.9	12261.7	+2.4	85.2	86.5	+1.5	1020893	1060519	+3.9

Assumptions: Area. Based on Table 7.1.

Relative productivity. 1975 estimate based on Johnson and Conway. 1990 estimate assumes that average productivity is increased by improvements on land not reclassified.

Weighted Product = Area x Relative productivity. The absolute numbers have no meaning. They can be to indicate changes in total product for each soil class or changes in the distribution of product between classes.

in class C land, it is of interest to calculate what effect this redistribution may have on agricultural output (Table 7.2). Here we have made the crude assumption that the index of productivity for classes A, B and C was 100, 80 and 70 respectively in 1975. The indexes are expected to rise as the result of farm improvements within classes to 102, 81 and 71 in 1990. The weighted product figures then take account of the change in total agricultural land, the changed distribution of land among classes, and the changes in average productivity per class as a result of land improvements. Our conclusion is that over the 15-year period, all these changes combined will only increase aggregate output by 3.9 per cent, about one-quarter of a per cent per year. The redistribution effect is neutral, the increased acreage causes about 60 per cent of the increase, and increased average productivity the remainder. This is in no way intended to disparage efforts at land improvement. It merely indicates that if land improvement takes place at the rate experienced in recent years and continues to be offset by losses of land to other uses, it will not have a major impact on aggregate farm output by 1990. Of course, heavy expenditure under CAP on land improvement schemes could alter this picture significantly.

The obvious next question, then, is what effect changes in labour and management applied to the available land may have on aggregate farm output in 1990. In Chapter 4 we showed how during the last decade, great advances have been made in delineating the factors which separate the more from the less productive farmers. We know that the better farmers tend to farm a larger acreage, to be younger and better educated than average, to have a longer planning horizon, better sources of information and urban standards of consumption, and to have what Johnson and Conway (1976) call good demographic structure, preferably being under 45, married, with young children living at home. It is not possible to trace values for all these variables through time. However, we can trace trends in the age, marital status and farm size of Irish farmers which should give us an indication of how the number and quality of Irish farmers is likely to change by 1990.

There are many ways in which one could attempt to project future populations of farmers. However, one must enter the caveat that all such projections are based on the assumption that some past influences on population will continue to affect populations in the same way in the future. For our purposes here, we use a projection by age of farmer and size of farm on the assumption that the average farm-non-farm income ratio in the next two decades will be the same as in the decade 1961–71 (Table 7.3). It will be as much as the Common Agricultural Policy of the EC can hope to offset the lower price and income elasticity of agricultural output relative to non-agricultural. Note that only male farmers are analysed by sub-categories. Most female farmers are farmers by accident rather than career choice, their numbers fell sharply in the 1961–71 decade, and are assumed to have the same proportionate decline in each decade to 1991.

Projections of numbers of farmers tend to be controversial both because the available data are ambiguous and because such projections involve assumptions about the

Table 7.3: *Male farmers by age-group and farm size, female farmers and total farmers,* 1971 *actual and* 1991 *projected*

Male farmers	1971 *Actual*	1991 *Projected*
numbers	162,980	152,346
Per cent by age group		
25 years	2.0	2.0
25–34	7.9	12.9
35–44	17.0	22.8
45–54	24.6	22.5
55–64	25.9	20.0
65–74	16.5	15.1
75 and over	6.2	4.7
Per cent by farm size		
<30 acres	33.7	27.1
30–50 acres	26.6	29.1
50–100 acres	26.5	29.0
100 and over	13.2	14.8
Female farmers		
Numbers	18,647	7,638
Total farmers		
Numbers	181,627	159,984

Source: Census of Population 1971, Volume IV. Authors' estimates.

continuation of past social and economic trends. Irish entry into the European Community, the EC transitional increases in Irish farm prices, the energy crisis, and world recession have made extrapolation of these trends into the future more difficult. While the farm-non-farm income ratio has improved since EC entry, we are assuming that once the transitional period ends in 1978, Irish farm incomes will become subject again to the powerful long-term forces which favour non-food over food demand. Accordingly, we would expect the number of male farmers to fall by about 10,000 and of total farmers by over 20,000 in the next two decades (Table 7.3). Projections of number of farmers by age and size of farm are complicated by the interaction between these factors. If we assume (reasonably) that all land which can be farmed will be, then the fewer older farmers who leave farming, the fewer the younger farmers who will be able to enter, and the smaller the average size of farm will be. Clearly, too, when an older farmer retires or dies, his land may either be operated by an heir or sold either to new entrants to farming or to existing farmers. In the aggregate over a decade, it is difficult to predict under what circumstances and how often such conflicts will result in new entry with no change in average farm size and farm numbers, or farm enlargement with an increase in farm size and a decline in farm numbers. The NESC study (1977) of the New Farm Operators gave some useful pointers. We assumed arbitrarily that the net land released in any farm size category would be available in other size categories in proportion to existing farm size. For example, for each 100 acres released in the under 30-acre category, 1/15 would be allocated to the under 30-acre category, 2/15 to the 30–50-acre category, 4/15 to the 50–100-acre category and 8/15 to farms 100 acres and over. Our assumption thus implies that larger farmers will have a comparative advantage in acquiring land that becomes available, a result that is likely on both theoretical and practical grounds.

The most notable feature of the projections is the large increase in the proportion of male farmers under 45 and the large decrease in the proportion of farmers on holdings of less than 30 acres. Average size of farm in each size category would increase. We can expect an increase of over 13,500 younger farmers and a decrease of over 13,500 small farms. However, the projections suggest that the social problems associated with small farms and aged farmers will persist. By 1991, there will still be 30,000 male farmers aged 65 or over, and over 40,000 farmers operating less than 30 acres. Ironically, it is likely that a worsening of the farm-non-farm income ratio would hasten the demise of smaller farms particularly on poorer western soils. However, unless off-farm employment was readily available, the departure of farmers would also mean the loss of entire families in rural areas with the attendant economic and social consequences for those who remained.

While it seems obvious that the improved structure of Irish agriculture would lead to output increases, any estimate of the likely size of these increases must be tentative. Other studies have suggested that the relative productivity of farmland varies with the age of the operator. If, as suggested by Conway (1975), farmers aged 45–64 had 75 per cent of the gross output per acre of farmers aged less than 45, and farmers aged 65 and over had 50 per cent, the transfer of land to the younger age-groups by 1991 would lead to an increase in gross output of 8.1 per cent. Clearly, reallocation of land to younger farmers will not alone greatly improve aggregate output. In addition, if farms in the 30–50 and 50–100 acre categories continue to be most efficient for the type of agricultural enterprise common in Ireland, any gains in efficiency from reduction of land in farms of less than 30 acres may be offset by losses from land transferred to farms with more than 100 acres. Some increase in output may arise as larger farms acquire more skilled labour units. There is some evidence of development of a new class of specialised agricultural worker. However, there is no information to indicate what the change in the number and allocation of agricultural workers by farm may be. Finally, cohort analysis suggests that about 30,000 males under 45 entered agriculture for the first time in the decade 1961–71. At that rate of entry, by 1991 about half of male farmers will have entered agriculture subsequent to

Ireland's entry to the European Community, and will have had access to managerial and technological knowledge not available to earlier generations of farmers. If the proportion of high-level management increased from one-quarter to one-half of all acres farmed between 1971 and 1991, and high level managers could achieve one-third higher output with the same resources, then this management quality change could increase aggregate output by a further 7.7 per cent by 1991.

The final determinant of the productive potential of Irish agriculture is the system of farming practised. The farmer can choose both the products he wishes to produce and his method of production. We have seen that the decline in tillage and the switch to cattle and dairying were justified by the resources and economic incentives available to Irish farmers in the last two decades. Irish agriculture is still heavily dependent on the natural fertility of its grasslands. To that extent, the population of livestock which can be maintained has a natural upper limit. Nature's capacity can be stretched to some degree. Fertilisation of pasture improves summer grazing. Conservation of pasture in the form of hay or silage, cropping of feed grains, or importing grain or protein-rich feeds can be used to increase supplies of winter feed. However, one cannot rob Peter to pay Paul. Grassland set aside for hay is removed from the grazing supply. It will only pay to transfer land from one use to another if the marginal value product in the new use exceeds that in the old. Imports run into a capital, not a land constraint. Increased imports in the long run can only be financed out of increased gross margins, which in turn depend on the price of inputs and outputs and the technical efficiency of transformation. Only the last can be to some extent controlled by the individual farmer.

In projecting conditions to 1990, we begin with the assumption that because of powerful existing economic forces Irish agriculture will have as its primary production goal the maximisation of output of livestock and livestock products, and that other forms of output will grow in so far as growth is compatible with the livestock sector. Increasing beef production has been a major policy goal for 20 years, while access to the EC market has stimulated new emphasis on dairying which has not yet been dampened by current surplus conditions. We take as our starting point the crop and livestock situation in June 1974 when the cattle cycle reached its greatest peak in the history of Irish agriculture. First, looking at the available acreage, we saw from Table 7.2 that total agricultural land may increase by 286,700 acres, only 105,000 of which will be in the wide use range category. Declines are not likely to contract crops such as malting barley or sugar beet or in fruits and vegetables. At the same time, while acreage of wheat, oats and fodder crops may decline, production is likely to continue on those farms where conditions are most advantageous. We have assumed that half the acreage of non-contract crops in 1974 can be released for other uses by 1990. Thus, a total of 449,450 additional acres could be devoted to pasture, hay, silage or feeding barley (Table 7.4). We have assumed that all the tillage land released would go to feeding barley, all the new class A land to silage and the new class B and C land to hay. Since the feeding barley would replace other crops which are used for feed, the actual gain in feed output at 1974 yields would probably be in the same range as the gain in acreage of hay and silage, that is, between five and 12 per cent. Assuming that winter feed is a greater constraint than summer pasture, and using estimated 1974 yields, we can estimate that the reallocation of land to hay, silage and feeding barley would increase domestic feed output by about 11 per cent. Since about one quarter of winter feed requirements have customarily been imported, the increase in domestic production would increase the cattle-carrying capacity of Irish agriculture by about eight per cent.

How might that cattle-carrying capacity be allocated in 1990? Of the estimated total of 8,028.7 thousand cattle, we assume that by 1990, because of the availability of winter feed, none of these would be held to over three years of age. If we assume the increase equally shared over all other classes of cattle so that the ratio of cows to heifers in calf, calves and cattle 1–2 years, remains as in 1974, and that 2–3 year old cattle increases to offset decreases in cattle over 3 years, we can estimate the numbers in each class in 1990. Total cattle numbers would be 11.3 per cent higher than in 1974. The 1990 cow population would sustain an annual output of cattle (based on the ratios established by Baker, O'Connor and Dunne, 1973) of 90 per cent of 2,393.5 thousand, or 2,130.2 thousand head.

Assuming 1974 prices and yields, the value of output of Irish agriculture would increase in the cattle sector by £58 million and in the dairying sector by £19 million. Increases in feeding barley output would likely be offset to a large extent by decreases in other displaced crops. Accordingly, if no decreases in output of pigs, poultry or sheep resulted, the increased capacity for cattle and dairying could by 1990 yield an increase in value of gross agricultural output of £77 million, an increase of 8.4 per cent.

It is important to note that these estimates of potential growth in dairying and cattle refer only to growth arising from diversion of land from crop to livestock uses. Up to this point, we have assumed yields constant at 1974 levels. Increases in yields of pasture, hay, silage and feed crops could directly increase the carrying capacity of a given acreage. Increases in yields of competing crops could permit release of more land for cattle-oriented enterprises. The sources of increased yield would include the use of fertiliser, improved seeds, herd improvements, better timing and conservation methods and the synergistic effects not previously measured of the combination of better land quality, farm size, skill of management and labour and new technology.

It is difficult to get a realistic measure of the aggregate effect of greater fertiliser use. For example, in field experiments Ryan (1974) has shown that the yield of pasture could be increased from 7.0 to 11.3 tons per hectare DM equivalent by use of 310 kg/ha of nitrogen. However, this sort of increase is unlikely to be achieved on all pasture acreage by 1990 for a number of reasons. Some farmers are already fertilising optimally, so their potential for further yield increases is lessened. Some land will not respond as effectively as test plots. Indeed, Walsh (1964) suggests that in certain cases, increased fertilisation may damage pasture or reduce the quality of grass

Crop acreage	1974 actual (1000 acres)	1990 projected (1000 acres)	Change 1974–90 (1000 acres)	(%)
Wheat	136.1	68.05	−68.05	−50.0
Oats	108.3	54.15	−54.15	−50.0
Barley, malting	159.7	159.7	–	–
Barley, feeding	448.3	648.05	+199.75	+44.6
Other corn crops	7.9	7.9	–	–
Potatoes	98.7	61.7	−37.0	−37.5
Turnips, mangels and fodder beet	81.1	40.55	−40.55	−50.0
Sugar beet	63.7	63.7	–	–
Other root and green crops	32.0	32.0	–	–
Fruit, etc.	8.9	8.9	–	–
Total crops	1144.8	1144.8	–	–
Grassland for hay	1693.4	1784.25	90.85	+5.4
Grassland for silage	854.3	959.3	+105.0	+12.3
Pasture	8282.5	8373.35	+90.85	+1.1
Total crops and pasture	11975.0	12261.7	+286.7	+2.4
Cattle numbers				
Cows	2151.3	2393.5	+242.2	+11.3
Heifers in calf	213.1	239.1	+24.0	+11.3
Bulls	17.2	19.1	+1.9	+11.0
Other cattle, 3 yrs. and over	211.2	–	−211.2	−100.0
2–3 years	1063.9	1418.7	+119.8	+33.3
1–2 years	1728.5	1923.1	+194.6	+11.3
less than 1 year	1829.3	2035.2	+205.9	+11.3
Total other cattle	4832.9	5377.0	+306.9	+11.3
Total cattle	7214.5	8028.7	577.2	+11.3

produced. McCarrick (1966) has shown that the effect of fertilisation is complicated by stocking rate and other considerations. In addition, from an economic point of view, increased fertiliser use will only be desirable if the marginal value product exceeds the marginal cost of the additional quantity used. That is, both the price of products like beef and butter and of the fertiliser itself, will determine the economic optimum. The same comment can be made about foodstuffs as has been made about fertilisers. While they can be used to increase yields, the level of use is dependent on the relative prices of the inputs and of possible outputs. However, unless the ratio of feedstuff prices to beef and dairy prices improves markedly from present levels, their impact on Irish yields is likely to be minimal. When the output increases in the years 1960–75 were allocated by source, the residual attributable to yield increases was 21.8 per cent (Table 7.5). Accordingly, we can reasonably assume that average yield increases would range from one per cent per year (say 15.0 per cent) to the 21.8 per cent achieved in 1960–75 in the next 15 years. It is estimated that a greater share of production marketed as output added 1.4 per cent to gross output in the 1960–75 period. Our projections assumed no growth from the source in the 1975-90 period.

Table 7.5: *Sources of growth in Irish agricultural output*, 1960–75 *estimates and* 1975–90 *projections*

Source	1960–75 estimated per cent	1975–90 projected per cent
Increased agricultural land area	+ 6.6	+ 2.4[1]
Land improvement (drainage, etc.)	+ 0.8	+ 1.5[1]
Entry of younger farmers	+ 4.2	+ 6.1[2]
Improved quality of management	+ 7.8	+ 5.8[3]
Concentration on cattle enterprises	+ 4.9	+ 8.0[4]
Yield increases	+21.8	+15.0–21.8[5]
Output marketed	+ 1.4	+ 0.0[5]
Total all sources	+47.5	+38.8–45.6

Sources: [1] Table 7.1.

[2] Table 7.3 and text disucssion, 8.1 per cent increase for 1971–91 prorated to 1975–90 period.

[3] 7.7 per cent increase for 1971–91 discussed in text, prorated to 1975–90 period.

[4] Table 7.4 and text discussion.

[5] See text discussion.

We can then summarise the potential for increased output from various sources. Over the fifteen years, 1975–1990, we can expect real output increases from all sources of 38.8–45.6 per cent as compared to a 47.5 per cent increase in the 1960–75 period. However, it is important to note that the largest single item, yield increases, is also the most problematical. One might also argue that the item for improved quality of management is partly included in the change to younger farmers and yield increases. Accordingly, it appears reasonable to assume that the maximum possible output increase will be somewhere in the 35–45 per cent range. It also appears realistic given past changes in gross output of Irish agriculture which were below three per cent per annum for the last two decades. Even if we assumed that yield increases would contribute as much to growth as in the 1960–75 period, the annual growth rate to 1990 would still be below three per cent.

Our estimates have assumed that the land-using enterprises will continue to dominate agriculture. It is, of course, possible that changes in the ratios of input prices to output prices may in the future favour non-land using enterprises such as pigs, poultry, yard-feeding of cattle, etc. It is also possible, but unlikely, that reductions in energy costs may make glasshouse enterprises more widespread or that growth of demand for potatoes, vegetables, etc., for processing may increase tillage acreage. In subsequent sections, however, it will become apparent that existing demand factors are unlikely to alter the pattern of output of Irish agriculture from its present course. Accordingly, the projections of supply in this section have an important bearing on the projections for the processing sector included in Chapter 13.

SECTION II

MARKET POTENTIAL TO 1990

Chapter 8

Preconditions for Market Expansion

I N the previous section, we suggested that Ireland can increase its output of agricultural products by about 2.2 per cent per year up to 1990. The next key question is whether it can find sufficient profitable markets for that increased output, or indeed if markets might grow even more rapidly (as some have suggested) so as to permit a breakthrough to even higher levels of output.

In order to achieve expansion in sales of the level envisaged, two preconditions must be met. There must be growth in the major markets in which Irish agricultural products are sold, and Ireland must be able either to maintain or increase its market share. One could, of course, envisage a situation where total market demand grew so rapidly that Irish sales increased even though Irish market share decreased, but there is little precedent for such growth in food sales over a long period. Alternatively, in a stagnant or declining market, Ireland could increase sales by increasing its market share. However, here again, the general experience of agricultural (and indeed all) marketing is that it is extremely difficult to increase market share on a declining market in view of the general excess capacity that prevails in such circumstances.

In looking at potential markets, we comment first on some broad issues that will affect demand for all commodities. Next, we look at the evidence available on the competitiveness of Irish agriculture relative to its main competitors for European and overseas markets. Then, we examine the current situation and prospects for the major commodities of interest to Ireland in its present main markets. Next, we present quantitative estimates of the volume of increased sales possible in these markets under assumed price and income trends. Finally, we look at changes in present policies which would be desirable if Ireland is to find profitable markets for all its output.

CSO estimates suggest that 42.8 per cent of the farm value of agricultural output in 1975 was sold on the domestic market. The distribution of sales of all milk products and of butter were close to this average. Crop, pig and sheep products were sold predominantly in the home market, but over 80 per cent of the output of cattle and calves and of cheese were exported. The United Kingdom took over a quarter, Northern Ireland about seven per cent and the rest of the European Community about 10 per cent of 1975 output. Thus, the 32 counties of Ireland together took half of all output and roughly twice that taken by the United Kingdom. About 90 per cent of all output was sold within the European Economic Community's protective shield. Even though, in 1975, Ireland was in its third year as a full member of the

European Economic Community, only its cattle and sheep and meat thereof had made significant inroads into the market of the original six members of the Community. In addition, the higher prices in the European Community had diverted some Irish agricultural exports from former third-country markets, so that almost all of Irish agricultural output had become sensitive to general economic and marketing conditions in the European Community and to Community-wide policies, in particular, the Common Agricultural Policy.

Some of the problems which were affecting Irish agricultural sales in the EC–9 in 1975 included generally low population growth, a reduction in immigration, low or negative income growth in the face of world recession, and record unemployment. More specifically in agriculture, there were large surpluses of beef, butter and skim milk at the prevailing support prices and consumer resistance to increased purchases at those prices. In addition, great uncertainty and intermittent distortions in trade arose because of the use of monetary compensatory payments to offset the effect of currency fluctuations in an attempt to preserve common agricultural prices. The CAP itself was subjected to varied criticisms both internally from the major food importers, the United Kingdom and West Germany, and externally from exporters such as Australia and New Zealand who resented exclusion from traditional markets, and importers such as the United States which regarded CAP export restitutions as contributing to dumping of dairy products on their market.

Clearly, then, the dominant factors likely to influence the market for Irish agricultural products in 1990 are the progress of the economies of Ireland, the United Kingdom and the remaining Community partners, and the evolution of the Common Agricultural Policy. While there were over 250 million people in the enlarged EC in 1975, the overall rate of population growth was expected to slow considerably in the next decade due to a declining birth rate and reduced immigration from third countries. Walsh's estimates suggest that the Republic of Ireland population could reach 3.7 million by 1990. The Northern Ireland population was expected to remain stable at 1.5 million, so that the total population of Ireland could be 11.8 per cent above 1975 levels in 1990. Official forecasts suggest that the UK population could increase by three per cent by 1990, that of the rest of the European Community by about 16 per cent, so that for the EC–9, the population would grow by less than one per cent per year.

It was expected that the recession of the mid-'seventies would be followed by a renewal of economic growth. However, no firm forecasts existed of the likely rates of growth. Accordingly, it seemed reasonable to assume that these would approximate the rates of growth actually achieved in the 1960–70 period when GNP *per capita* grew by approximately four per cent in the EC–9 (excluding the UK) and 2.8 per cent in the UK. Allowing for the, as yet uncertain, contribution of North Sea oil, we rounded the UK growth rate up to 3.5 per cent, the rate projected by the most recent OECD study for the 1975–80 period. Together, these estimates for population and income suggests that GNP in the Community and in Ireland will almost double by

1990, that in the UK will increase by two-thirds. Such optimistic projections will only be achieved if economic growth can be maintained fairly consistently with the minimum of adverse shocks over the 15 year period. However, in general, the economic environment should be favourable up to 1990.

It is doubtful if the environment for Irish agricultural products will be quite so favourable. Numerous commentators (see Fennell's survey, 1973) have pointed out that price supports set under CAP in recent years have tended to boost production retarding consumption so that costly surpluses have been built up. Accordingly, the EC Commission itself has been forced to take sporadic measures to reduce output, the latest being the Action programme which aims to bring supply and demand for dairy products into line by 1980. In products such as beef, where surpluses are less common, the EC's commitments to the Lomé Convention and special trade agreements with developing countries requires the admission of some imports. In sugar, the EC is committed to import 1.4 million tonnes of cane sugar, or about 10 per cent of annual production. In these products, the goal of increased income for EC farmers must be weighed against broader trade and strategic considerations. The prices for meat and for cereals have tended to be delicately balanced so that pig production based on cereals cannot be expanded rapidly. Any weakness in pig meat prices or increase in feed costs, therefore, can injure all but the most efficient pig producers. The absence of a common policy in mutton and lamb and potatoes has discouraged producers from these enterprises. A further barrier to an effective common agricultural policy has been the instability of exchange rates between major EC currencies. Green (i.e., agricultural) rates of exchange were permitted to lessen the impact of changes in official rates of exchange, but were used differently by different partners, in some cases to aid farmers, in others to protect consumers, so that the one price system effectively broke down. To prevent price distortions, CAP used monetary compensatory payments which themselves created trade distortions. The sum total of actions has been the antithesis of a common market in agricultural products regulated by the forces of competition. However, as EC Commissioner, Haferkamp, wrote in 1976, diverging monetary values merely reflect the deep economic divergencies between member countries. The Community will need a lot of luck and farseeing policy initiatives if it is to secure economic convergence by 1990. Chances are that bouts of monetary instability will recur in the meantime.

In summary, then, the future market for Irish agricultural products in the EC–9 will not be as buoyant as would have been the case if the favourable conditions prior to Ireland's accession had persisted. In a subsequent section, we review the prospects by market and commodity. However, it is relevant to suggest here that under most likely conditions and assuming constant 1975 real prices for agricultural products, Ireland will not be able to find a market within the Community for all it can produce by 1990. It has then two alternatives, either to find new markets outside the Community or to try to work to change the CAP and other related policies so as to expand its market within the Community.

We will discuss the potential in European Community markets in more detail later. At this stage, it is sufficient to point out some of the possible opportunities and problems of expanded extra-Community sales. In the past, the major problems facing Ireland in third country markets has been the protectionism, low income levels, or inadequate foreign exchange of the importing countries, excessive competition from many suppliers chasing the free world markets, inadequate marketing organisation of Irish export sales, and undeveloped taste for Irish agricultural products. Adolf and Ernst Weber (1975) have predicted an "explosion" in the demand for animal protein in developing countries "as soon as the basic energy requirements for metabolic processes and work performance have been met." A number of countries have shown remarkable growth in income *per capita* in the last decade and are already demanding a higher proportion of animal protein foods in their diets.

These countries fall into a number of groups based on their source of income growth and foreign exchange reserves. In a category by itself is Japan which has developed industries under native control, capable of exporting advanced industrial goods to advanced countries and willing to permit selective access to its protected food market in return for continued access for its exports. A number of other countries have become havens for multinational companies which find their tax laws, cheap labour and other inducements attractive as a springboard for sales to the advanced country markets. This group includes Taiwan, Korea, Singapore and Hong Kong, which are already major importers of temperate foodstuffs. A further group has gained an enormous boost in both income and foreign exchange earnings from the operation of the oil cartel of the Organisation of Petroleum Exporting Countries. Since it appears that the OPEC cartel can hold the real price of oil at approximately present levels, these countries have a unique opportunity to base development on their own resources. Initially, much of the oil revenue has been channelled into investment in economic and social infrastructure, but as higher incomes become more widely distributed the content of imports is likely to change from emphasis on producers' capital goods to consumer goods including food. Of present OPEC members, Indonesia and Nigeria are the fifth and ninth most populous countries in the world. The 12 OPEC countries have a population equal to that of the EC–9. Chile, Colombia, Mexico and Mainland China, which have had large oil finds since 1973, may experience similar growth to the OPEC group in the future.

A number of advanced countries could become important outlets for temperate food products, particularly where the land for extensive cattle-raising is limited, for example, Sweden, Switzerland and Austria. A further group of small countries or territories have *per capita* GNP equal to, or greater than, that of Ireland, as a result of their close links with developed countries. Included are Bermuda, Puerto Rico, the US Virgin Islands, French Polynesia and New Caledonia.

It is likely that there will be many examples of rapid income growth and growth in food consumption throughout the world by 1990. However, there are many question marks over whether or not these opportunities can be converted into profitable, commercial markets for Irish agricultural products. The US market is likely to remain protectionist in its attitude unless some mutual reduction of protection can be agreed with the European Community. As long as these two major importers remain protectionist, the world's major non-aligned agricultural exporters, e.g., Australia, New Zealand and Canada, will be forced into the few remaining free markets with depressing effect on prices. The profitability of free markets and their size is likely to vary with the phase of the world cattle cycle and the world supply of cereals. A repeat of the world food shortages of 1973–74 whether due to excess demand as in beef, or crop failure as in cereals is possible for brief periods during the rest of the century.

Clearly, it will be difficult to build up a stable demand for Irish agricultural products in third countries under such erratic market conditions. The European Community has tried to offset the effect of changing world price levels by the use of export restitutions. However, where one Community member has established commercial markets in third countries and another member has not these restitutions can become a cause of lower world prices, can arouse violent opposition among competing producers, and can unfavourably discriminate between exporters from member countries. Certain initiatives already under way may, within the next decade at least, lead to more stable rules of the game in international trade in food. The developing countries have been vociferous in condemning the impact of volatile price swings in commodity agreements in various international forums. The Carter administration in the US has come out in favour of commodity agreements in wheat and other products critical to world food supplies. As the European Community itself now has the capacity to be a consistent net exporter of a number of food products, its policy makers may become more willing to negotiate with the US and other major exporters on trade arrangements for agricultural products, perhaps linked with comparable arrangements for other strategic materials such as uranium.

International arrangements negotiated by the Commission of the European Community either for broad market access, or for bilateral deals, such as sales of intervention butter to the Soviet Union, may be directly competitive with the marketing efforts of Irish agricultural exporters. Clearly, then, Irish operations must be co-ordinated with Community-wide actions. Perhaps the first step to such co-ordination is that the Community should develop an explicit policy towards the export of agricultural products on a commercial basis to third countries. It seems unlikely that Ireland alone could finance the market intelligence, product development, sales and promotional operation needed to exploit developing market opportunities, for its increased production, especially if access was to be erratic because of political considerations, whereas the Community as a whole could fund such a marketing effort. On the other hand, while it would be more difficult for Ireland to go it alone in third country markets, any benefits gained would not have to be shared with other EC partners. However, more and more of international trade is now subject to political deals between major trading blocs. For the long run, as the next section suggests,

Irish interests may best be served by ensuring that the negotiating stance of their bloc, the European Community, is one that permits access for certain Irish products to third country markets on a competitive basis.

How Competitive is Irish Agriculture?

In view of its importance to expansion of sales of Irish agricultural products either within the EC or in third countries, amazingly little hard data are available on the competitiveness of Irish agricultural producers and marketers. Frequently, competitiveness has been assumed even in such critical situations as the negotiations prior to the Anglo-Irish Free Trade Area Agreement and before Ireland's accession to the EC. The general assumption has been that Ireland was competitive with other EC partners in the production of live animals, beef and dairy products, therefore, after entry should be able to increase its market share of such products. However, if Ireland is to market its increased output potential, competitiveness will become an absolute necessity for success. Competitiveness will be particularly important if the growth of Irish sales has to be at the expense of rival suppliers.

Within the time limitations of this project it has not been possible to develop a rigorous analysis of the competitiveness of Irish agriculture. In the next few paragraphs we draw together fragmentary data bearing on the issue. However, it is necessary to point out that competitiveness can be defined in a number of overlapping ways; is rarely the sole criterion for business or Government decisions, and tends to alter over time. Competitiveness may be measured in terms of absolute cost advantage, comparative cost advantage, changes in market share, ability to survive under adverse conditions, technical and managerial efficiency and other factors. A firm or country may have an absolute cost advantage but not a comparative cost advantage. In turn, neither cost advantage may generate sufficient income or other benefits so that it can be fully capitalised upon. Over time, the supply curves of different sets of producers will shift at different rates so that when they are selling in a single market some producers will become extra-marginal while others will be able to enter the market or expand production at a profit. Accordingly, the evidence cited below is intended to be indicative rather than conclusive about the competitiveness of Irish agriculture.

It has been generally assumed that Ireland has an absolute advantage in the production of livestock or livestock products because of the high grass content and the low proportion of purchased feed used in production. However, New Zealand has a longer season for grass and requires less winter housing. A USDA study of suppliers of dairy products to the US market indicated that New Zealand could deliver butter to US ports at about half the cost of major EC suppliers. A study by Horan (1975) suggested that Irish costs of raw materials and processing were almost double those of New Zealand, that, is, comparable to major EC competitors. In livestock and beef production, the evidence of history suggests that whenever Ireland has been granted fair access to major markets, sales have surged. The absolute level of cost has been kept low by considering land as free, by internal financing of cattle stocks and by rise of the farmer's own and his family's generally unpaid labour. If most production costs were cash costs as they are on the many farms in the UK and elsewhere where the farmer is a tenant paying rent, interest on borrowed funds and wages to hired labour, Irish costs of livestock production would appear higher and might exceed those in other countries.

While it is not possible to provide evidence that Ireland has an absolute cost advantage in the production of milk and beef, Josling and Lucey (1972) used estimates of historical supply and demand curves to show that in the enlarged EC, Ireland would have a comparative advantage in these products while the UK should specialise in grain, and Denmark in pigs. The basis of that comparative cost advantage would lie in the availability of forage and labour and in Ireland's location near the large UK deficit market for beef and dairy products. Whether that comparative advantage would persist as Ireland expanded its output is a moot point. Generally, increased milk production has been achieved by increasing the stocking rate of cows per acre through use of more fertiliser, increased making of silage and purchases of supplementary feeds. Demand projections for the UK suggest only sluggish growth in the next decade. So, while Ireland will probably continue to have a comparative cost advantage in milk and beef production within the EC, the profitability of that advantage might be reduced somewhat.

Recorded changes in market share reported in a subsequent section suggest that Ireland is more competitive in beef than in dairy products. In general, dairy product sales have been expanded through either political or institutional arrangements, especially in the UK market. Bord Bainne have recognised this fact by promoting sales of Irish butter as a premium (ergo, higher priced) product. In contrast, Irish beef tends to sell at a discount in the UK market, but has been very successful in expanding market share on continental EC markets. However, Weinschenck (1973) has maintained that changes in market share within the EC have kept within relatively small limits because the CAP has tended to support prices above domestic market equilibrium and thus impeded the growth of interregional competition. Effective regional competition, he said, was least likely to take place on the grain, milk and beef markets. In that light, then, expansion of the Irish beef market share is probably indicative of Ireland's competitiveness in that product.

Some indication of competitiveness is also evident in the ability of different groups to survive adverse market conditions without Government aids. The Irish cattle industry has demonstrated the ability to survive and grow in all kinds of market situations. Partly this is because of the element of self-exploitation mentioned already. When prices are low so that the use of purchased feeds cannot be justified, the Irish cattle producer has been able to rely on natural forage to remain in business, while reducing payments to his own land, labour and capital. However, there is a limit to this competitiveness. When farmers cannot tolerate further reductions in living standards they go out of business. The greater becomes the indebtedness of the remaining Irish cattle producers to banks and other outside sources of finance, the less easy it will be to survive by low-input production methods.

Perhaps the most controversial aspect of the competitiveness of Irish agriculture relates to its level of technical and managerial efficiency in production. We have suggested previously that the level of technology used prior to EC entry was partly that which was justified given the often surplus, low-price conditions on the UK market. Yields have increased fairly steadily in both crop and milk production. However, milk continues to have a low fat content and to vary widely in quality. Conway estimated that the volume of net product per man increased by 23.6 per cent in the 1953–73 period. Perhaps least responsive to change was the beef cattle industry which remained heavily dependent on traditional systems of production, namely, reliance on the seasonal availability of grass, maintenance winter feeding and long maturation of production. For example, only 29 per cent of the 1–2 year-old cattle in the United Kingdom on June 1, 1974 survived to June 1, 1975, whereas the comparable survival rate in Ireland was 76 per cent. Thus, Ireland needed an additional winter of feeding to finish its cattle, required a greater total cattle herd for a given annual output, and had a much slower turnover of capital invested in stock. Indeed, in 1972–74, the output of beef per 1,000 head of cattle was (at 55 tons) the lowest in the European Community. Increasing the output of grass per acre under Irish climatic conditions poses many complex technological problems. The alternative approach of speeding up the production process by supplementary feed usage tends to neutralise the possible cost advantages from use of cheap grass.

The surest way to capitalise on Ireland's natural advantages in grass production is to find methods of increasing grass output with the minimal use of other inputs. The desirable long-term economic situation would be, *not* the maximum production of grass, but the maximum added production for the minimum added inputs. However, there is little evidence that Irish agriculture is willing to go in this direction.

The only exhaustive attempt of which we are aware to compare Irish agriculture with that of a major competitor is the NESC study on Dutch agriculture by Murphy (1976). Murphy found that during the period 1956–1973 Dutch agriculture had consistently higher output per man and per acre for crops and milk than Irish agriculture. While Irish crop yields had grown at about the same rate as those of the Netherlands in the period, the yield of grass per acre and of milk per cow had grown faster in the Netherlands. Value added per male permanent worker was more than three times that achieved in Ireland. Even though Dutch farmers injected a greater volume of capital and purchased inputs and had a lower value added per unit of output, this was more than offset by the extremely high level of output. One outcome of this has been that in 1972–73, the most recent year for which data were available, GDP per person employed in Dutch agriculture was 87.7 per cent of that outside agriculture, whereas the comparable figure for Ireland was 55.2 per cent, with West Germany the lowest in the EC. These statistics would suggest that within the EC, Ireland and West Germany still have some unexploited comparative advantage in utilising more of the agricultural labour force in non-agricultural employment.

The foregoing, admittedly superficial, examination of the evidence on past and present competitiveness of Irish agriculture is only modestly encouraging. Looking to the future, there is little evidence that Irish agriculture can easily catch up with New Zealand, Holland or Denmark which themselves are under constant pressure from rising costs to improve their level of technology and managerial efficiency. Furthermore, within the EC, Ireland's locational advantage in the UK market could be seriously eroded if income growth in the UK lags that of other EC markets. Of course, it may be argued that competitiveness with New Zealand and other third country suppliers is irrelevant if they can be excluded from the EC market by political decisions, and if surplus output can be sold into intervention. We turn to discussion of future market opportunities in the next section.

Chapter 9

Demand by Commodity

J UST as in the case of output potential, so it is important to attempt to quantify what future demand for the output of Irish agriculture may be under alternative assumptions. However, to set the stage for quantitative estimates market by market it is useful to review the current situation and prospects of the leading Irish food products in existing markets. Because of the relative importance of the different commodities our discussion is divided into five categories,

(a) beef and cattle
(b) mutton and lamb
(c) dairy products
(d) pork and bacon
(e) all other products.

These groups accounted for 42.9, 3.3, 26.0, 7.2 and 20.6 per cent, respectively, of all Irish agricultural output and 60.6, 1.9, 26.6, 2.6 and 8.3 per cent of agricultural exports in 1975.

Use of these categories is forced on us by the manner in which official statistics are kept. However, the reader should be aware that the types of channels in which a product is sold (retail, catering, etc.), the product form (frozen, chilled, canned, etc.),

Table 9.1: *Importance of different categories of meat in world production and exports*

Meat	Production average 1969–71 per cent	Exports 1970 per cent
Beef	40	50
Sheepmeat	7	14
Pork	36	27
Poultry	17	9
Total meat	100	100

Source: UN FAO. Review of meat production and demand projection to 1980.

the different levels of investment involved, the growth prospects of the market (expanding, stable, contracting) may be more meaningful in assessing future demand.[1]

Beef is the most important type of meat in terms of total production, consumption and international trade, followed in turn by pigmeat, mutton and lamb and poultry meat (Table 9.1). Given its agricultural product mix, Ireland is well placed to benefit from the importance of beef in total meat exports and could become a major exporter of sheepmeat. Since pork and poultry production are non-land using enterprises, they can be located near major markets so that international trade takes place in the cereal and other feed inputs rather than in the meat products. As long as this situation continues, the opportunities for increased international trade in pork and poultry meat will be limited.

(a) Beef and Cattle

Even though about 3.3 million farms, occupying 60 per cent of EC acreage, are engaged in beef production, the EC until 1974 was not self-sufficient in beef. The surpluses in that year have accentuated the decline in cattle numbers as a result of the peaking of the cattle cycle simultaneously in many countries (Table 9.2). However, cattle census results now becoming available for 1976 and 1977 suggest that cattle herds have stablisied throughout Europe. The next peak in the cattle cycle may occur about 1982 and the subsequent one about 1990. Accordingly, there is no reason to expect that the intervening years will be more stable than the recent past during which the EC has swung from shortage and soaring consumer prices to surpluses and price slumps. A feature of high price periods has been a plateau or, in the case of the United Kingdom, an actual decline in the volume of beef consumed. However, it is impossible at this point to tell whether this reflects a temporary or an actual shift in consumer tastes.

Table 9.2: *Production of beef and veal from indigenous animals in EC countries*

Country	1969–71 average (1000 tonnes)	1972–74	1974	1975
		Base 1969–71=100)		
Belgium	243	100	121	116
Denmark	225	91	109	108
France	1646	101	114	113
W. Germany	1266	98	108	106
Ireland	342	108	131	164
Luxembourg	14	93	100	100
United Kingdom	957	102	113	127
Italy	805	93	98	73
Netherlands	293	100	123	127

Source: UN, FAO. Production Yearbook.

[1]Based on a comment by Dr. P. J. Loughrey on an earlier draft.

OECD estimates of future meat consumption in Western Europe under alternative assumptions of zero growth or past growth in *per capita* consumption give a range for 1985, of from 28 to 36 million tons. OECD rejects the maximum figure as failing to take account of signs of consumer saturation and the minimum figure as disregarding the large potential increases in Southern Europe where the rate of increase in both beef and veal and pigmeat in the last two decades has been twice that of their Northern neighbours. OECD estimates that production of beef and veal could increase in Western Europe at between 1.5 and 2.5 per cent annually to 1985. Whether consumption can increase as rapidly will depend both on the trend of incomes and on the future changes in taste, including the, as yet, unpredictable impact of soya products and other meat substitutes. A realistic view would be that growth in consumption will tend to lag behind that in production rather than vice versa.

Given this likely scenario for overall EC supply-demand balance, what are the prospects for Irish producers of beef and veal and live cattle? It is not possible, and indeed would be misleading, to suggest that a simple answer exists to such a question. International trade statistics show that where trade barriers are removed, the flow of live cattle, beef and veal in Western Europe follows an intricate and varied pattern, with countries alternating as exporters and importers, or acting simultaenously in both roles depending on their needs for final products and for livestock at intermediate stages for further production. Trade in calves and other live animals tends to be between neighbouring countries and for reasons of stock building or replacement, and for utilisation of spare capacity in grassland, feedland, feedlots or slaughter houses. However, within the EC system a movement of calves from Germany to Italy in one year may stimulate an increase in cow numbers in Germany in the following year and a demand for Irish beef *to fill the subsequent gap in beef production* two years later. Another common feature of trade is the reverse flow of different parts of the animal. For example, France exports forequarters and imports hindquarters. Within markets so diversified by language, custom and tradition as those of Western Europe, the size of carcase, conformation, type of cut, marbling, packaging, etc., demanded, can vary widely between neighbouring regions. Accordingly, choices made at time of breeding and at all stages of production can serve to influence the eventual price and market opportunities for the final product.

Irish exporters of live cattle, beef and veal have increased their share of the total EC market from 16 per cent in 1969–71 to 23 per cent at the height of the production cycle in 1975 (Table 9.3). Increases in France, Germany and the Netherlands have been even more spectacular, largely at the expense of Eastern European suppliers, although caution is needed in interpreting these figures because the proportion which were shipments into intervention in 1975 is not known. However, note the large increase in Irish market share in the traditional United Kingdom market. The future is likely to be influenced as much by political as by economic conditions. The United Kingdom still appears keen to reduce the imported share of its food needs, but may have less leeway for continuing the policies of the last decade within the EC CAP.

Relations with Eastern Europe may influence how liberal a policy the Community wishes to adopt towards extra-EC imports. It will remain difficult for Ireland to choose the best possible breeding, production and processing policies for beef and cattle as long as both commercial markets and the Community's future policies are uncertain.

Table 9.3: *Irish share of European Community live cattle, beef and veal imports, 1969–71 average and 1975*

| | Irish share of imports (per cent) | |
	1969–71	1975
European Community	16.0	23.0
France	0.1	13.9
W. Germany	0.4	21.5
Italy	0.2	3.3
Netherlands	0.5	20.0
United Kingdom	53.0	70.0

Source: UN, Economic Commission for Europe. European Market for meat and livestock, 1975 and 1976.

One of the continuing controversies of the Irish cattle industry is whether live cattle exports should be stimulated, merely endured or actively discouraged. At issue is the potential employment and value added which could be generated by slaughtering all Irish cattle in Ireland. We will return to this issue in a subsequent section. What can be said is that the European market for live animals (and in particular the United Kingdom market) is still very much alive and well, and there is no indication that it will disappear unless the major importing countries themselves take deliberate steps to eliminate it.

(b) Mutton and Lamb

The recent history of the Irish mutton and lamb trade has been an unhappy one. Much sheep production has been squeezed out of lowland producing areas by cattle expansion and mutton and lamb products out of the major United Kingdom export market by domestic supplies. Since entry to the EC, sales to continental Europe have increased. While the annual live equivalent of all exports of live sheep, mutton and lamb in the 1974–76 period declined by about 320,000 head compared to the 1964–66 period, and sales to Great Britain declined by 386,000 head, the increase in all other markets represented only 66,000 head. France, a large deficit market for mutton and lamb, blocked efforts to have those products included under CAP because such freeing of trade would weaken its ability to protect its own producers, but gave Irish products limited access to the French market under a 1977 agreement. The future of the export trade to continental Europe is, therefore, more than usually dependent on political and legal battles yet to be fought. In the meantime, sheep raising is likely to continue to expand only in hill and mountain areas where it is at least disadvantage relative to cattle raising.

(c) Dairy Products

World milk production has been increasing in recent years, but, as one might expect, the consumption of liquid milk has stagnated. Except for Japan where *per capita* whole milk consumption had traditionally been low, major countries experienced either a decline or limited growth in the twelve-year period to 1974 (Table 9.4).

Table 9.4: *Consumption of whole milk per CAP. (Base 1962=100)*

	1962	1965	1970	1974
France	100	95	75	66
Germany	100	92	101	95
Belgium	100	92	89	82
Denmark	100	99	89	77
USA	100	99	88	82
Japan	100	142	193	204
Italy	100	103	108	103
UK	100	103	103	106
OECD (Excluding Turkey, Yugoslavia)	100	99	95	91
Canada	100	94	86	86

Source: Ireland: Bord Bainne Annual Report, 1975.

Table 9.5: *Consumption of cheese per CAP. (Base 1962=100)*

	1962	1965	1970	1974
France	100	120	150	152
Germany	100	120	142	161
Belgium	100	109	137	158
Denmark	100	100	108	113
USA	100	108	129	149
Japan	100	300	700	900
Italy	100	94	113	119
UK	100	100	117	130
OECD	100	105	125	141
Canada	100	114	150	188

Source: Ireland: Bord Bainne Annual Report, 1975.

While liquid milk consumption has declined products like cheese have enjoyed increasing popularity not only in developing countries but also in the North American and European markets. Table 9.5 shows a constant increase in *per capita* consumption of cheese in the ten selected areas. However, Table 9.5 does not show the widely differing levels of *per capita* consumption of cheese. France's consumption of 15 kg per head in 1974 was two-and-a-half times that of the UK and over four times that of Ireland.

Table 9.6: *Consumption of butter per CAP.* (1962=100)

	1962	1965	1970	1974
France	100	111	112	111
Germany	100	97	100	81
Belgium	100	86	95	91
Denmark	100	94	87	85
USA	100	88	73	64
Japan	100	300	400	600
Italy	100	127	133	147
UK	100	100	99	98
OECD	100	96	91	85
Canada	100	104	89	74

Source: Ireland: Bord Bainne Annual Report, 1975.

Butter and ghee ranked second to cheese in terms of world production. Table 9.6 shows for the same areas how butter consumption has changed over time. Consumption of butter has fallen on a *per capita* basis in most OECD and EC countries. Consumption has fallen most heavily in Germany which has been the prime market for Irish exports among the original EC-6.

The marked decline in butter consumption in the developed countries can, in part, be attributed to the competition from a powerful substitute (margarine). However, it remains to be seen whether the other determinants of demand which come into play, e.g., income, population, price and food habits, can offset the effects of butter substitutes. The slow but consistent decline in overall EEC butter consumption is of special interest to Ireland, since traditionally almost 70 per cent of Irish milk has been used for the production of butter or its derivatives. The emphasis over recent years has been to diversify milk utilisation – to ensure that less and less emphasis is placed on butter and more on the production of the other dairy products. However, Griffith-Jones (1977) has shown that since 1971, Irish milk has been increasingly concentrated in the two EC intervention products, butter and skim milk powder.

Irish skim milk powder production and exports have experienced rapid growth in the last decade. Factory-produced skim milk powder has taken the place of liquid skimmed milk which was largely returned to the farmer. It has tended to replace whole milk powder in the production of instant milk powder, ice cream, confectionery, chocolate and other foods, and is also used for animal feed. Exports in 1974–76 were on average more than ten times those of a decade earlier. However, a decision of the EC Commission in late 1974 which permitted subsidised sales out of intervention in third country export markets undermined Irish commercial export sales. As a result, about 40 per cent of production, over 50,000 tonnes of Irish skim milk powder, were sold into intervention in 1975 and 1976. However, Irish intervention stocks accounted for only five per cent of the over one million tonnes of total EC stocks of skim milk powder. A major goal of the EC Action programme for dairy products is to reduce stock levels to more manageable proportions. Accordingly, the opportunities for further increases in production of skim milk powder for exports may be limited until EC supply and demand comes more into balance. While the EC Action programme aimed to restore that balance by 1980, foot-dragging by individual Governments and the Council of Ministers may permit the imbalance to continue into the mid-1980s. The EC may be willing to tolerate continued use of intervention if the total volume or cost of stocks remains close to present levels.

Of the 674 million gallons of milk taken into Irish creameries in 1976 approximately 200 million were consumed in manufactured form on the home market and the balance exported to over 80 countries throughout the world. The UK, our main market for dairy products, is also Europe's major importer of butter and cheese (Table 9.7). The relatively small size of the Irish dairy export industry is made obvious by Table 9.8. It is also apparent from Table 9.8, how heavily Irish exports of dairy products are weighted towards intervention products.

The high-price support policy for milk under CAP has been a primary cause of the slowdown in sales of consumer products such as butter and of products for further processing such as chocolate crumb and casein. Their future fate appears to be primarily dependent on CAP decisions. Efforts by Irish dairy industry leaders to encourage diversification by pooling the costs of producing non-intervention products face an uphill battle as long as the financial resources of CAP favour intervention products. There is also a serious question mark over the ability of the Irish dairy industry to develop, test and successfully mass market new dairy products. While agencies such as Bord Bainne, (the Irish Dairy Marketing Board) can for a time squeeze additional returns out of a limited budget, in the long term, Ireland must be able to maintain an acceptable minimum of marketing effort including mass consumer advertising, if it is to maintain a branded franchise. The current structure of the industry is so weighted that investment in marketing for long-term benefits is sacrificed in order that processors can compete for milk supplies by offering marginal price advantages to producers. Ironically, these milk supplies are then diverted to intervention products. A continuation of this structure will make it extremely difficult for the Irish dairy industry to diversify into new markets and new products.

Table 9.7: *Imports of butter, cheese and skim milk powder*, 1973 *and* 1974

Into:	Butter '000 tons		Cheese '000 tons		Skim Milk Powder '000 tons	
	1973	1974	1973	1974	1973	1974
Belgium	91.1	81.0	59.4	63.2	37.9	42.6
France	25.8	23.9	38.1	15.8	8.9	3.6
Germany, Fed. Rep.	39.7	30.1	170.6	175.0	9.1	18.1
Italy	41.8	51.6	143.8	150.2	227.8	215.0
Luxembourg	..	..	..	..	..	..
Netherlands	18.0	12.2	13.0	15.8	181.1	206.3
United Kingdom	332.8	447.1	135.2	122.9	15.6	24.5
Austria	0.8	1.3	4.5	5.9	0.9	0.9
Spain	0.8	1.6	4.6	12.3	38.6	42.5
Sweden	0.1	0.1	10.5	11.8	0.2	0.7
Switzerland	15.4	12.4	19.7	20.8	2.2	2.1
Czechoslovakia	0.7	0.3	0.7	0.7	..	..
German Dem. Rep.	29.5	17.0	13.4	8.5	..	..
Poland	..	..	0.7	0.6	0.3	0.4
USSR	226.1	10.9	7.5	6.9	20.7	21.7
Canada	1.4	2.4	19.3	21.8	1.9	1.7
Mexico	2.5	7.9	0.7	1.2	45.2	90.6
United States	22.9	6.3	96.6	140.9	119.0	78.5
Brazil	6.3	2.0	0.4	0.2	14.3	13.5
Chile	3.0	3.0	0.2	0.3	19.7	59.1
Peru	10.9	10.2	0.3	0.8	28.2	23.6
Algeria	6.0	8.5	10.3	4.9	10.8	24.6
Lebanon	4.0	3.9	8.9	8.9	4.9	8.4
Morocco	5.0	9.7	2.9	2.9	2.3	3.4
Japan	18.1	24.5	38.0	45.9	57.0	85.2
Philippines	4.3	3.7	3.9	3.7	59.1	57.7
Australia	..	..	8.1	7.2	0.5	1.2

.. Not available

Source: Ireland: Bord Bainne Annual Report, 1975.

Table 9.8: *Exports of butter, cheese and skim milk powder, 1973 and 1974*

From:	Butter '000 tons 1973	Butter '000 tons 1974	Cheese '000 tons 1973	Cheese '000 tons 1974	Skim Milk Powder '000 tons 1973	Skim Milk Powder '000 tons 1974
Ireland	44.7	35.2	38.5	46.1	105.8	68.3
Belgium	93.8	78.0	11.0	13.9	72.5	74.6
Denmark	80.0	90.4	82.8	93.2	75.1	79.1
France	182.9	90.0	158.1	160.6	223.3	221.3
Germany, Fed. Rep.	119.6	150.5	80.6	99.9	197.4	176.2
Italy	—	—	21.4	26.3	0.3	0.4
Luxembourg	..	..	..	..	..	..
Netherlands	179.6	179.0	206.3	226.8	47.4	72.6
United Kingdom	12.6	3.5	6.1	11.9	112.6	49.6
Austria	2.8	3.7	26.6	29.7	17.3	19.6
Finland	11.3	19.0	22.8	22.3	0.3	27.0
Norway	0.4	0.2	17.0	17.7	1.9	0.1
Spain	—	..	0.1	0.1	14.8	0.4
Sweden	9.0	12.2	3.4	3.0	16.8	17.3
Switzerland	—	—	50.7	50.9	3.3	2.3
Bulgaria	1.9	1.7	17.0	11.3	—	..
Czechoslovakia	5.6	4.9	8.1	9.1	—	..
German Dem. Rep.	1.5	..	..	..	..	..
Hungary	1.5	3.8	7.7	7.7	..	4.9
Poland	22.9	38.4	3.4	6.0	2.6	8.5
Romania	9.5	11.8	9.9	10.4	..	..
USSR	17.2	18.0	7.4	7.6	1.2	1.0
Yugoslavia	..	..	0.5	..	..	..
Canada	—	—	5.3	3.7	119.5	57.7
Mexico	—	—	—	—	..	..
United States	1.5	0.3	3.2	3.4	4.6	3.0
Brazil	7.5	0.1	0.2	0.5	—	—
Colombia	—	—	—	1.7	0.2	0.2
Japan	—	0.3	—	—	7.6	3.3
Australia	61.5[a]	32.1[a]	37.4[a]	33.7[a]	94.9[a]	..
New Zealand	157.7[a]	161.6[a]	68.4[a]	64.2[a]	212.1[a]	111.9[a]

[a] Year ended June 30 of following year.
— Negligible or zero.
.. Not available.

Source: Ireland: Bord Bainne Annual Report, 1975.

(d) Pork and Bacon

As pointed out earlier, pigmeat tends to be produced near major markets under factory type conditions and relying heavily on internationally traded feed inputs. Since demand changes only slowly, cycles in pig production tend more and more to be triggered by cycles in the supply and price of feed inputs. The international trade in pigmeat is disturbed even more by these cycles, since for most countries the domestic market is the main outlet and export markets take up the residual demand. Trends in Irish pigmeat production have brought greater intensification and dependence on compound feedstuffs, so that the Irish cycles are likely to come more and more into phase with the rest of the EC. The very sharp swings in the volume of Irish pigmeat production are reflected in even sharper swings in the export residual (Table 9.9). For example, in 1972, 45 per cent of Irish pigmeat production was exported, in 1975 only 20 per cent. Such fluctuations make development of a stable consumer franchise in export markets extremely difficult.

Sales of pigmeat in the domestic Irish market as well as in the main export outlets have fallen in the 1969–75 period. Gross exports of live pigs, bacon and ham to Western Europe as a whole are estimated by the UN to have fallen by 66 per cent in the same period. Prospects for a recovery of export sales are dependent both on the likely trend of *per capita* consumption and on Ireland's ability to increase its market share. Recent trends in *per capita* consumption for selected countries are presented in Table 9.10. Future pigmeat consumption will also be influenced by the trend in availability and price of cereals and other inputs, and of beef and veal and other final products. Apart from a limited franchise for Irish bacon products in the United Kingdom market, most exports of Irish pigmeat are based on competitiveness in price. Such a market can only be maintained on the basis of competitiveness in costs, something which becomes increasingly difficult as the industry becomes more dependent on imported feeds. In terms of consumer preference, the United Kingdom bacon market is dominated by Danish and UK suppliers. Denmark has made large inroads into other West European markets, so that an increased market share for Irish pigmeat products on a non-price basis at the expense of Denmark would require heavy investment in new product development, marketing and sales promotion. The present structure of the Irish pigmeat industry does not make this feasible. Pork exports have been successfully expanded in the Japanese market, but are vulnerable to any increases in domestic supply which would get preferential access. Accordingly, the Japanese market does not as yet offer any long-term stability on which to base a large expansion of Irish pigmeat production.

(e) Other Products with Export Potential

While the successful increase in exports of beef, dairy and pig products is vital to absorption of the increased output of Irish agriculture by 1990, there may be opportunities for increases in exports of some minor products. A healthy trade has grown up in the export of malt products from malting barley. This business is conducted

Table 9.9: *Production of pigmeat in selected countries* 1969–75

Country or Region	1969–71	1972–74	1974	1975	1975 *as* % *of* 1974
Austria[a]	286	316	330	335	102
Belgium	488	625	672	629	94
Denmark	743	780	758	745	98
Finland	108	126	125	128	102
France	1,312	1,491	1,510	1,535	102
Germany, Fed. Rep.	2,603	2,643	2,710	2,752	102
Ireland	145	144	131	97	74
Luxembourg	10	9	10	9	90
Netherlands	708	850	916	938	102
Norway	66	76	77	77	99
Sweden	235	272	280	286	102
Switzerland	201	231	237	235	99
United Kingdom	944	980	979	817	83
North-western Europe	7,849	8,543	8,735	8,582	98
Greece	56	90	107	108	101
Italy	544	653	676	736	109
Portugal	90	116	117	140	120
Spain	468	586	710	602	85
Yugoslavia	306	347	393	390	99
Southern Europe	1,464	1,792	2,003	1,976	99
Western Europe	9,313	10,335	10,738	10,558	98
of which European Economic Community (9)	7,497	8,175	8,362	8,258	99
Bulgaria[a]	182	208	194	301	155
Czechoslovakia[a]	528	623	632	662	105
German Dem. Rep.[a]	828	963	1,024	1,114	109
Hungary[a]	274	547	617	632	102
Poland[a]	1,300	1,749	1,888	1,782	94
Romania[a]	455	611	638	651	102
Eastern Europe	3,667	4,701	4,993	5,142	103
Europe (excluding USSR)	12,980	15,036	15,731	15,700	100
USSR	3,938	4,860	4,650	4,887	105

[a] Estimated by FAO.

Source: UN FAO, Production Yearbook.

Table 9.10: *Apparent consumption of pigmeat per head in selected countries*
(kg)

Country	1969–71	1972–74	1974	1975	1975 *as %* *of* 1974
Austria	32.5	36.7	37.5	38.2	102
Belgium	33.6	40.0	43.0	41.7	97
Denmark	30.2	33.5	32.6	36.5	112
Finland	20.1	24.3	25.0	28.0	112
France	30.8	33.0	33.2	33.9	102
Germany, Fed. Rep.	39.1	42.2	43.6	44.2	101
Iceland	2.0	2.5	2.8	2.8	100
Ireland	30.3	30.7	30.6	24.5	80
Netherlands	27.2	28.9	30.1	31.7	105
Norway	17.7	19.6	20.8	20.5	99
Sweden	26.1	28.9	30.7	32.2	105
Switzerland	32.8	36.4	36.9	36.9	100
United Kingdom	22.9	22.4	21.4	18.8	88
Greece	6.2	10.1	11.9	12.0	101
Italy	12.8	16.1	17.2	18.1	105
Portugal	10.4	14.5	14.7	16.7	114
Spain	14.0	18.0	20.4	18.2	89
Yugoslavia	13.5	16.7	19.1	17.8	93
Bulgaria	17.5	21.5	21.7	n.a.	n.a.
Czechoslovakia	32.0	36.3	36.6	38.1	104
German Dem. Rep.	40.1	45.2	46.2	47.8	103
Hungary	29.9	36.0	37.8	41.2	109
Poland	32.8	39.3	39.4	40.9	104
Romania	17.9	23.3	23.7	22.6	95
USSR	16.2	18.2	18.8	19.2	102

Note: Apparent consumption in terms of carcase weight (excluding slaughter fats and edible offals) of all animals slaughtered in the country, plus net imports (minus net exports) of pork, bacon and ham. No reference is made to stored quantities nor to foreign trade in pigmeat products other than bacon and ham. The figures may therefore differ somewhat from national sources.

Source: UN FAO, Production Yearbook.

with large multinational brewing companies who have considerable flexibility in where they draw their supplies, and through merger, trade agreements, etc., can obtain increased control of marketing outlets in many countries. Sugar exports to Northern Ireland could also increase depending to some extent on the relative costs of transportation of refined sugar to Northern Ireland from suppliers in the United Kingdom and in the Republic of Ireland, in part on the economies of scale available to UK producers, and in part to the marketing strategy adopted by different factories. The political decision on access of sugar cane from developing countries may upset this projection. Potato exports could also increase to Northern Ireland, Northern England and Scotland. However, such an expansion would require large-scale industry investment in quality control, grading, packaging and brand promotion. The Irish Sugar Company has made a number of attempts to sell vegetable products at various stages of processing in the United Kingdom market but has been handicapped by insufficient supplies, inadequate distribution or both. Expansion of exports of processed vegetables would probably not occur unless economic circumstances favoured a trend towards increased tillage. Past trends in consumer demand and current CAP pricing policies have consistently pulled Irish agriculture in the opposite direction.

General Comment

Output of the main livestock products produced by Irish agriculture is heavily influenced by the nature of the systems and processes of production used. The type of products which can be marketed are limited by the breeds of animals that are raised and by the needs of other EC markets which have evolved separately over many centuries. Ireland's output is not large enough to supply all types of different products required by this complex market, so it must select those markets on which it can most profitably concentrate. However, only in the case of some dairy products does it have the organisation to market branded consumer products and even there it is handicapped by the conflicting pressures of CAP and by its own lack of finance. Irish exports must compete against well-organised, multinational food companies which dominate the food markets of most European countries. It is doubtful if any single Irish industry, cattle, dairy or pigmeat, can alone marshal the resources to hold the mass markets in which it must now compete, never mind expand effectively into new markets. Clearly, enormous (relative to past efforts) investment in marketing would be needed by the Irish agriculture and food industry to change that situation. The current CAP system does nothing to encourage such needed investment. While it tends to stimulate production of raw materials, it encourages processing of intervention products and discourages through high price of raw materials, the needed diversification into new or minor products. Our best projections suggest that by 1990 the situation will still be that of too much food production chasing too little consumption throughout Western Europe. Ireland is likely to face the same problem of excess production, especially in its traditional products. However, such a pessimistic situation in 1990 is not inevitable. The Irish agricultural industry could marshal its resources more effectively than it presently does and could gear itself to take advantage of new marketing opportunities as they arise. In the next chapter we attempt to quantify the markets which Ireland might be able to capture under alternative assumptions.

Chapter 10

Future Demand in Major Markets

WE turn now to projections of 1990 demand for Irish agricultural products in major markets under alternative assumptions about the growth of population and *per capita* incomes. Since demand for Irish food products is determined by so many external or uncontrollable (by Ireland) economic and political factors, it is not our intention to present exact predictions or to suggest that these patterns of demand will emerge irrespective of what actions Irish agriculture takes. However, it is important to give policymakers some feel of the order of magnitudes involved. Of course, to be most effective, this sort of projection should be updated on a regular basis as new developments, new initiatives or new information appear.

Demand projections face enormous problems of data availability and accuracy. We have drawn heavily on the pioneering projections of FAO and OECD of food demand to 1985, and have attempted to push these forward to 1990 with the aid of more recent worldwide data and studies of individual countries. We have assumed that the major determinants of future food demand will be growth in population and *per capita* income. In general, we have assumed that the real price of each food will remain constant to 1990, there will be no change in the relationship between the products under study and actual or potential substitues, and no change in Government policies affecting food demand. To do otherwise would have made the study unmanageable in size. Of necessity then we have had to assume away any long-term effects of TCAs, MCAs, consumer subsidies and other measures which have caused temporary distortions in intra-EC trade. In subsequent discussion, we speculate about the effect of relaxing some of our assumptions. For ease of comparison, markets are quantified in terms of the proportion of 1975 Irish agricultural output which they have absorbed or could absorb by 1990 (Table 10.1). Data were not available on all markets and all products. However, Table 10.1 is sufficiently detailed for our present purposes.

For convenience we discuss potential markets within the EC in three categories:

(1) Territorial Ireland, including the Republic of Ireland and Northern Ireland.
(2) Great Britain.
(3) The remaining European Community and its associated territories.

In addition, we discuss, but do not quantify, other possible markets.

(1) *Territorial Ireland.* Clearly, within a fully harmonised European Community Common Agricultural Policy, territorial Ireland would become the home market

95

Table 10.1: *Proportion of 1975 agricultural output sold in major markets, 1975 actual, and 1990 projected*

Output category	Republic of Ireland		United Kingdom[1]		Other EC[2]		United States		All Other[5]		Total	
	1975	1990	1975	1990	1975	1990	1975	1990	1975	1990	1975	1990
Cattle and Calves	7.9	12.7	11.6	12.8	8.0	12.0	0.3	1.8	15.1	15.1	42.9	54.4
Butter	5.5	6.5	7.4	9.1	[3]	[3]	[3]	[3]	1.5	1.5	14.4	17.1
Cheese	0.9	2.2	3.3	3.9	[3]	[3]	[3]	[3]	0.1	0.1	4.3	6.2
Other Milk	4.2	5.8	1.2	1.2	[3]	[3]	[3]	[3]	1.9	1.9	7.3	8.9
Sheep and Lambs	2.2	3.3	[3]	[3]	0.6	0.9	[3]	[3]	0.5	0.5	3.3	4.7
Pigs	5.7	10.0	0.8	0.8	0.1	0.2	[3]	[3]	0.6	0.6	7.2	11.6
Sugar beet	1.9	2.1	0.6	0.6	[3]	[3]	[3]	[3]	0.2	0.2	2.7	2.9
Potatoes	2.4	1.5	[3]	[3]	[3]	[3]	[3]	[3]	0.2	0.2	2.6	1.7
Other	11.4	11.4	[3]	[3]	[3]	[3]	[3]	[3]	3.9	3.9	15.3	15.3
Total	42.1	55.5	24.9[4]	28.4[4]	7.6[4]	13.1[4]	0.3[4]	1.8[4]	24.0	24.0	100.0	122.8

Sources: Agricultural Output and Exports; Irish Statistical Bulletin, June 1976. Exports: Trade Statistics of Ireland, 1975.
[1]Excluding Northern Ireland.   [2]Original EC-6 and Denmark.   [3]Insufficient data.   [4]Excludes all other.
[5]Assumed constant

for producers both North and South. For example, in mileage terms, the cities of Belfast and Derry are nearer to Dublin than Cork city. Producers in the Republic of Ireland could gain an increased share of the Northern Ireland market and vice versa. The main factors affecting the sales in Ireland of Republic of Ireland producers in 1990 will be the changes in total population, incomes and food purchasing habits and the relative competitiveness of Republic of Ireland, Northern Ireland and foreign producers.

By 1990, at a growth rate of 1.1 per cent, the population of the Republic of Ireland will have reached about 3.7 million, that of Northern Ireland may stabilise at about 1.5 million, giving a total population of Ireland about 11.8 per cent above 1975 levels. National income *per capita* in Northern Ireland in 1975 was about £1,170 compared to £925 in the Republic of Ireland. If the growth rates achieved in the 1960–70 decade could be maintained to 1990, income *per capita* would rise to £1,878 in Northern Ireland and £1,620 in the Republic, for an overall gain in *per capita* income of 68.5 per cent. Of course, unforeseen population and income trends could cause a wide divergence from this figure. However, there is a likelihood of substantial increases in consumers' purchasing power in Ireland by 1990. Using the estimated expenditure elasticities reported by O'Riordan for the Republic of Ireland, an increase of two-thirds in *per capita* incomes would increase *per capita* demand for milk, cheese, beef, mutton and pigmeat, but not for butter, sugar or potatoes. Growth of population and *per capita* incomes in the Republic of Ireland of the order envisaged above would require Republic of Ireland farmers to produce an estimated 13.4 per cent greater output than they did in 1975. Details of the estimated change by output category are shown in Table 10.1.

In Northern Ireland, a smaller and less rapidly growing population would not offer as large a total growth as in the Republic. Furthermore, Northern Ireland is itself a net exporter of all the products listed above with the exception of sugar. It is possible that greater economies of scale may emerge in the beef and dairy processing industries in the Republic of Ireland *vis-à-vis* Northern Ireland. However, other competitive factors may offset this advantage. What is most likely is a rationalisation of production and marketing areas so that North and South achieve greater efficiency without greatly altering market shares.

Perhaps a more serious threat to selling increased output on the home market will be the competitive inroads of other EC suppliers. There is no way of predicting at this point in time what inroads will be made on the Irish market by 1990 by French cheese, Dutch butter, Danish bacon, etc. Much will depend on the future changes in the EC's Common Agricultural Policy and on changes in comparative cost advantage. Accordingly, the prospect of the Irish territorial market absorbing a 13.4 per cent output increase over 1975 levels by 1990 might be considered a maximum target which would be adjusted downwards if population or income *per capita* grew more slowly than planned, or Irish producers lost some of their dominance in the home market.

(2) *Great Britain.* Prospects for sales of Irish agricultural products in the British market are dampened by the expected slow rate of population growth (about three per cent in 1975–90), the slow economic growth (unless oil revenues greatly stimulate growth during the 1980s) and the weak response of *per capita* food consumption to increases in income. An OECD assessment of growth in total real output suggested an annual growth rate for the United Kingdom from 1975 to 1980 of three and a half per cent given a five and a half per cent growth for all OECD countries. United Kingdom imports (excluding oil) would be expected to grow at eight and three quarter per cent annually, about the same rate as all OECD countries. A lower growth for all OECD countries would reduce the United Kingdom growth rates. The achievement of the modest three and a half per cent growth was conditional on inflation being reduced from around 16 to six per cent, a process not evident in 1977 trends. The emergence of North Sea oil and gas in the 1980s may permit the attainment of real growth on a par with other OECD countries. However, the United Kingdom is unlikely to experience growth in real *per capita* incomes exceeding three and a half per cent per annum for the 1975–90 period.

Using the most recent estimates of income elasticities derived by Mitter (1975), the suggested rates of population and income growth would indicate growth in total United Kingdom demand over the fifteen year period to 1990 of about 10 per cent for beef and veal, four per cent for bacon, and two per cent for butter and cheese. However, Great Britain will remain a major food importer and so of vital concern to Irish agriculture. The critical issue will be whether Ireland can hold or increase its market share.

The record over the past decade suggests that the Republic of Ireland has gained market share in Great Britain for its dairy products, has retained its share of the cattle and beef trade by substituting dressed beef for live exports, but has lost market share for pig and sheep products. Increased British production has reduced opportunities for Irish beef (in live or dead form) pork and bacon, while demand for mutton and lamb in total has fallen. Despite lagging demand and increased domestic production of butter and cheese, the Irish market share of these products has increased dramatically as non-EC suppliers were cut out after the United Kingdom's entry into the European Community. A further boost to Irish butter exports would follow any phased reduction of New Zealand's continuing access to the UK market for 100,000 tonnes of its butter. Some growth in Irish butter and cheese sales to Great Britain may also arise from the increased involvement of multinational food companies in the Irish dairy industry. Sales of skim milk powder may not reach record 1975 levels again for some years. An increase of sales by 1990 of 10,000 tonnes each of butter and cheese in the British market and maintenance of Ireland's share of the British beef market would require a 3.5 per cent growth in Irish agricultural output over 1975 levels. In view of the uncertainty surrounding the British market in general, such would be a reasonable marketing goal.

Given this low growth potential, the continued heavy dependence of some of the

Table 10.2: *Quantity of selected Irish agricultural exports to Great Britain, other markets and total markets and share of total exported to Great Britain, annual average 1964-66 and 1974-76*

Product	Unit	1964-66				1974-76			
		Great Britain Quantity	% of	Other Quantity	Total Quantity	Great Britain Quantity	% of	Other Quantity	Total Quantity
Live cattle	No.	442,701	65.9	229,119	671,820	224,642	44.6	279,533	504,175
Bullocks, fat	,,	72,733	54.6	60,356	133,089	653	1.9	33,495	34,148
Bullocks, store	,,	252,313	69.3	111,841	364,154	168,983	57.6	124,527	293,510
Live Sheep, lambs	,,	21,385	8.8	220,845	242,230	1,305	8.8	142,593	143,898
Beef and veal	tonnes	30,205	51.0	29,059	59,264	90,710	41.9	125,766	216,476
Mutton and lamb	,,	10,281	66.1	5,268	15,549	1,142	11.4	8,874	10,016
Pigmeat	,,	9,376	74.3	3,251	12,627	943	11.6	7,201	8,144
Bacon and ham	,,	27,096	97.1	802	27,898	13,222	91.5	1,232	14,454
Butter	,,	12,040	57.6	8,848	20,888	39,919	73.1	14,694	54,613
Cheese	,,	10,235	91.9	897	11,132	48,033	90.1	5,300	53,333
Dried milk	,,	8,148	49.1	8,460	16,608	31,441	25.6	91,418	122,859
Beer	1,000 bbl.	813	75.6	263	1,076	632	64.2	352	984

Source: Trade Statistics of Ireland, selected years.

main Irish agricultural products on the British market is a cause for grave concern. Irish beef, bacon, butter and cheese have been geared so long to the needs of British distributors and consumers that the system of production and processing has become relatively inflexible (Table 10.2). However, changing market orientation, for example, to woo German, Japanese or African customers, may require substantial changes in animal selection and breeding, feeding, timing of slaughter, processing and presentation. Some of the problems involved in such adaptation will be discussed in subsequent sections.

(3) *European Community.* The remaining members of the EC–9, the original six and Denmark, enjoyed a real growth in *per capita* incomes in the 1960–70 decade of four per cent or greater. OECD projections indicate the possibility of a similar rate being achieved in the 1975–80 period. At this rate, *per capita* incomes could more than double in the 1975–90 period. The slowing of population increase and the redistribution of population towards the older age groups will also affect the total size of the market and the type of foods that will be in increasing demand. If population were to grow at the 1960–70 rate (one per cent annually) it would increase by about 16 per cent between 1975 and 1990. Given the decline in birthrates experienced recently, and recent declines in entry of migrants this is probably a high estimate of population increase. Up-to-date evidence on income elasticity of demand for the main agricultural products of interest to Ireland is fragmentary. However, there is considerable consensus that the income elasticity for butter is close to zero, that for beef and veal, mutton and lamb and pork about 0.3 and for cheese about 0.5. Given the population and income figures mentioned above, one could expect by 1990 relative stagnation in total butter demand, an increase of about 50 per cent in the markets for beef and veal, mutton and lamb, and pigmeat, and of about 75 per cent for cheese. If Ireland could retain its 1975 share of European meat markets (which would be quite an achievement) its sales growth in these products would by 1990 amount to 4.4 per cent of 1975 agricultural output. (The Cooper and Lybrand 1977 study for the IDA suggested that growth of production in the EC–7 could increase the competitive resistance to Irish beef and cattle exports in the next decade.) Irish efforts to break into the European cheese market are still in their infancy and face formidable competition from established brands and varieties. Ireland will also suffer from locational disadvantages *vis-a-vis* its major competitors in the Community in serving continental Europe. Accordingly, we have assumed no measureable growth in sales of dairy products.

Clearly, the existing continental EC markets are not likely to provide exceptional growth opportunities for Irish agriculture. However, all four States on the verge of membership, Greece, Portugal, Spain and Turkey, have experienced high growth rates, are normally deficit areas for either meats or dairy products, have a large combined population (92.3 million in 1974) and much higher income elasticities of demand than current EEC members. The OECD projections for 1985 suggested that these four countries would need to import 416,349 and 91,000 tonnes, respectively, of beef and veal, mutton and lamb and butter-fat. Ireland's opportunity to supply some of that deficit would be increased if these countries were inside the EEC and Irish exports were not limited by tariff or other barriers. A 20 per cent share of these markets for Ireland in 1985 would in beef and veal be the equivalent of an added five per cent of 1975 Irish agricultural output, in butter three per cent and in mutton and lamb a further four per cent. However, such an increase in the mutton and lamb market would require a doubling of the present Irish sheep flock and would not be compatible with simultaneous increases in cattle production. Some proportion of these gains might be achieved even if none or only some of these countries became members of the European Community by 1990. Given the difficulties to be experienced in traditional Irish markets, greater emphasis on Southern Europe might be very rewarding to Irish food exporters.

Summary of Projection for EC Markets

Our projections, based on fairly generous assumptions about population and income growth in the face of constant real prices for food products and little growth in Ireland's market above 1975 levels, indicate that 21.3 per cent greater output of Irish agricultural products can be absorbed in Community markets in 1990 and an extra 1.5 per cent under favourable trade terms in the United States. In an earlier chapter we suggested that by 1990 Irish farmers could produce 38.8–45.6 per cent more. Accordingly, even allowing for considerable overestimates of output or under-estimates of demand growth, at constant real prices there seems a high probability that Ireland could produce more than it could sell, and an even chance that the surplus could be very large. In addition, the burden of absorbing increased production would fall most heavily on the Irish market, North and South, which by 1990 will be vulnerable to surplus production from other EC producers. The second most important market would continue to be the lagging economy of Great Britian. The other seven EC countries would still only take about half the volume of Irish agricultural products absorbed by Great Britain, even though their share would jump by about a half. While the CAP intervention system could temporarily absorb small surpluses, it seems unlikely that it could, on any long-term basis, absorb each year 10 per cent or more of total Irish agricultural output.

How serious the excess supply from Ireland would be would depend on whether Ireland alone had a surplus or whether all member countries had an equivalent percentage surplus. The Irish surplus, 16.0 per cent of 1975 output, would be only 0.32 per cent of 1975 Community output. Even if all the surplus was concentrated (as seems likely) in milk products, it would amount to less than 2.0 per cent of 1975 Community milk output. The question, then, is what reduction in price would be needed for the market to absorb this amount. Mitter estimated the price elasticity for dairy products in the UK at $-.0242$. O'Riordan's results suggest a weighted average value for Ireland of about $-.08$. It is likely that because of their phase of development, the remaining EC countries have price elasticities in the intervening range, say −.05. Accordingly, to absorb 2.0 per cent greater milk output in the Community, the real price of milk products would have to fall by 40 per cent! However, it seems most unlikely that the dairy industry in eight other EC member countries would agree to such a price reduction to enable Ireland to dispose of its surplus. As Oskam and Wierenga (1975) point out, their revenue would be increased by the opposite situation, a reduction in quantity marketed and an increase in price.

However, it is much more likely that the Community in total, and not just Ireland, will have a surplus of dairy products in 1990 if real prices remain constant and CAP and other economic policies are not changed. The most recent OECD forecast for the decade to 1985 reaffirms the EC Commission's forecast of a growing gap between production and consumption. In 1975, the EC Commission estimated production of milk at 91.7 million tonnes against consumption of 85.4 million tonnes. By 1985, production is forecast at 105 million tonnes and consumption at 78 million tonnes. Given that between 1968 and 1975 the Commission had to dispose of 10 per cent of butter production and 75 per cent of skim milk production, in powder or liquid form, at reduced prices, the potential drain on Community funds and the political resistance to such expenditure is likely to increase. While some increase in Irish sales of dairy products into intervention might be countenanced, intervention could not handle the enormous new burdens likely to be imposed upon it.

What is the likelihood of a real decline in the price of milk and dairy products? In fact, by 1976 this had actually begun in all EC member countries except Italy. The EC Commission recommended, and the Council of Ministers approved, price increases which were less than the general rate of inflation. The same may have occurred in a number of member countries in 1977. Real price decreases have been relatively modest so far and while cow numbers have dropped slightly, suggesting some supply response to lower prices, increased yields per cow have continued to boost production. Since three-quarters of all community milk producers still own fewer than 10 cows, real price cannot be reduced rapidly without meeting violent resistance from dairy farmers. The price cut necessary to reduce production is probably politically infeasible at present. However, the principle of declining real prices has been established.

Other measures could reduce the dairy surplus problem. Some have already been proposed or implemented by the Commission, converting dairy to beef herds, suspending national and community aid to the milk sector, increasing free milk for schools, encouraging use of skimmed milk for animal feed, taxing vegetable and marine oil and fats, etc. Ireland might also press for the extension of price supports to cheese as well as butter and skim milk so as to encourage diversification of Irish production into that section of the market which alone has been growing. Enlargement of the EC by admission of Southern European members could also boost demand for dairy products, even though it might increase surpluses in other commodities. Consumer subsidies could also be continued as a device to maintain producer price while stimulating consumption.

However, these measures are often contradictory in their effects and rarely get to the real issue which is that the common prices administered by CAP drew excess resources into dairying. Ultimately, it would appear to the authors that the only long-term solution is to allow dairy product prices to move closer to free market levels. CAP should now be attempting to move the dairy industry to a point where such a step could be taken without sudden disastrous consequences for any group of producers. A return nearer to free market pricing would benefit consumers with lower prices and a reduction of inflation, it would release resources from wasteful uses (including a large share of the Community budget), and it would encourage the free movement of agricultural products within the Community – which is, after all, one of the central goals of economic integration. The effects in agriculture would be a decline in the number of producers, some diminution in income for those who remained, but a considerable expansion in volume of products both for further processing and for final sale as production moved from intervention products to those products for which demand was most elastic, e.g., cheese.

A USDA study of the possible effects of free trade policies on the world dairy market indicated that net farm cash incomes of representative farms would fall by 13 per cent in Belgium, 20 per cent in Wisconsin, US, 28 per cent in New York, US, 30 per cent in France and 54 per cent in the Netherlands where dairy farming is most intensive. Net farm cash incomes would almost treble in New Zealand and increase by one and a half times in Australia. Within the EC, Ireland could expect that a reduction in milk prices would tend to hit its more intensive competitors, e.g., the UK and the Netherlands, most hard, part-time farmers especially in W. Germany would tend to go out of dairy production and within Ireland the least efficient producers would be eliminated. Thus, under a free market system, the proportion of Irish dairy producers surviving should be well above the Community average, the Irish share of the total EC market would be likely to increase as its comparative advantage in dairy products was allowed free rein, and the surviving farmers would be larger and more efficient, with higher output and income per farm.

Such a free market system would also benefit Ireland in third country markets. Each additional gallon of milk produced by an inefficient producer in the EC or US under price protection is a gallon less which can be supplied by efficient internal or external producers, and in effect a gallon more dumped on the residual world market. In our projections (Table 10.1), we have assumed no growth in sales of Irish agricultural exports in third countries excluding the United States. Under free trade, Irish exporters would be in a position to compete effectively on third country markets. The EC cannot, on its own, mandate free trade in world markets. However, it could take an important step in that direction by doing all in its power to encourage free trade within its own borders.

SECTION III

PROCESSING POTENTIAL TO 1990

Chapter 11

Irish Food Processing – General Characteristics

M ANY aspects of the Irish food processing industry have been thoroughly analysed in numerous previous studies. Study groups organised by the Department of Agriculture examined most food processing activities in preparation for the first attempt by Ireland and the UK to join the European Economic Community in the early 1960s. More recently, the prospect of accession in 1973, and the subsequent national unemployment problems, have brought renewed interest in the Irish food processing sector including studies by Baker *et al.*, Keane, Igoe, Murphy *et al.*, Quinn and Smith, O'Connell, the Industrial Development Authority, Bord Bainne, the Confederation of Irish Industries, etc. Our intention in this section is not to duplicate the work of these authors but to highlight the characteristics of the Irish food processing sector which are most relevant to projections of future output and employment.

Census of Industrial Production preliminary reports for 1973 show the relationship between food and drink processing industries and all Irish manufacturing industry in that year (Table 11.1). For convenience we will refer to individual industries by their popular name rather than their official designation in the CIP. The entire milling industry is included in the food sector even though a substantial proportion of its output is in the form of animal feed. About a quarter of all Irish manufacturing establishments in 1973 were engaged in food processing, a further three per cent in drink production. The number of persons engaged and net output per establishment was smaller in the food industry and larger in the drink industry than in all manufacturing. However, the differences between industries were more startling. Average employment ranged from 30 in milling to about 474 in the sugar industry and from 20 in malting to 648 in brewing. Net output per person, which is a crude measure of an industry's ability to compete for workers in the labour market was approximately the same in the food industry as in all manufacturing but more than twice that level in the drink industry. Net output per person was below the food industry average in the canning, confectionery, baking and miscellaneous food industries where lower-paid female labour was more prevalent.

No data on size distribution within industries were available for 1973. However, a CIP special analysis for 1968 showed that 52.8 per cent of food establishments and 41.3 per cent of all manufacturing establishments had less than 15 persons engaged. The incidence of small establishments was above the food industry average in the

Table 11.1: *Ireland, food and drink processing and all manufacturing industry, 1973*

	Official CIP designation	*Short title*	*Establishments* (No.)	*Persons engaged per establishment* (No.)	*Net output per establishment* (£000)
1.	Bacon factories	Bacon	37	124.3	437.5
2.	Slaughtering, etc. of meat other than by bacon factories	Meat	45	94.2	430,5
3.	Creamery butter, cheese and other edible milk products	Dairy	157	49.1	215.8
4.	Jams, jellies, preserves, etc. canned fruit and vegetables	Canning	32	105.0	282.2
5.	Grain milling and animal feeding stuffs	Milling	156	30.2	126.2
6.	Manufacture and refining of sugar	Sugar	4	473.8	1991.5
7.	Cocoa, chocolate and sugar confectionery	Confectionery	32	152.5	355.3
8.	Bread, biscuit and flour confectionery	Baking	273	33.9	86.3
9.	Margarine, compound cooking fats and butter blending	Margarine	7	63.6	329.3
10.	Miscellaneous food preparations (including fish)	Miscellaneous	58	29.3	77.8
11.	Distilling	Distilling	9	37.8	232.7
12.	Malting	Malting	18	20.0	127.7
13.	Brewing	Brewing	7	647.9	5786.3
14.	Aerated and Mineral waters	Soft drink	57	40.2	204.0
	Total Food (1–10)	Food	801	53.4	184.6
	Total Drink (11–14)	Drink	91	82.7	621.1
	Total food and drink	—	892	56.4	229.1
	Total manufacturing	—	3211	63.3	216.8

dairy, milling, baking, miscellaneous and soft drink industries. At the other extreme, only 11 food firms employed more than 500 persons. Only in the bacon industry had more than half of all establishments a gross output exceeding £750,000. Many other food industries had a dual character with one or a few large establishments and many small establishments.

No industry-wide data are available on the number of firms operating more than one establishment in the same industry or in different food industries. However, National Prices Commission studies of the flour milling and animal feedingstuffs industries indicated the importance of multi-establishment enterprises in both these industries. It is known, too, that many dairy firms have diversified into feed compounding, engineering, retailing, etc. Accordingly, firms in the Irish food industry have greater financial strength than would be apparent from CIP data on establishments. However, as we will discuss later, many firms which are large by Irish standards, are not so by the standards of international food processing.

The picture which emerges from the most recent data, therefore, must be regarded only as a snapshot in time of a sector which is evolving dynamically. Since 1953, the number of food establishments has fallen by over a quarter, but the average number of persons employed per establishment has risen by 63.3 per cent and the output per person employed by 47.9 per cent, so that total volume of production has risen by 78 per cent. In contrast, the number of all manufacturing establishments fell only slightly, and average number of persons employed rose less rapidly than in the food industry (45.9 per cent), but productivity rose by 95.3 per cent so that the volume of production of all manufacturing rose by 178 per cent in the 1953–73 period. Both the food sector and all manufacturing have experienced the same tendencies towards larger establishment size and continuous, mechanised and standardised production using imported technology. However, the income elasticities in a growing economy have stimulated the demand for non-foods much more rapidly than for foods. Since the same phenomenon has been experienced in all EC economies, the Irish food processing sector is unlikely to grow as rapidly as other manufacturing to 1990 unless it can capture some of the processing business which would otherwise be done in other countries. O'Connell pointed to the same phenomenon but did not speculate on its cause. We suggest that the slower growth rate in food processing has been due to the slower growth of final demand for food. Had productivity per worker increased in the food industry as rapidly as in all manufacturing, employment in the food industry in 1973 would have been below 1953 levels rather than approximately 7,000 greater even with a 78 per cent increase in volume.

Over the twenty-year period, 1953–73, the meat, dairy, canning and miscellaneous food industries have experienced growth in output volume greater than that for all food. In the case of the two former, export market expansion has been the main stimulus, while the two latter have been able to meet the needs of Irish consumers for variety in food consumption often using imported raw materials. In the drink sector, the soft drink industry, which grew fourfold since 1953, benefited from the growing between-meal snack and youth markets. While the number of meat, canning, and miscellaneous establishments had grown slightly since 1953, the number of dairy and soft drink establishments have fallen in line with all other food establishments, partly due to rapid growth in establishment size and partly due to increases in labour productivity. The processing of liquids such as milk and soft drinks has proved especially amenable to mechanisation and automation techniques.

While no sector of the food industry experienced an actual decline in volume of production between 1953 and 1973, the baking, confectionery, sugar, margarine, bacon and milling industries have grown relatively more slowly as has the brewing industry in the drink sector. Over-capacity has been a serious problem, alleviated somewhat by the declining number of establishments, but accentuated by the larger average size of plants and the introduction of output-increasing technology in the surviving establishments. Employment actually fell in the milling, sugar, confectionery and baking industries and in distilling, malting and brewing, all of which involve continuous, long runs of standardised products. Productivity per worker in distilling and malting increased almost fivefold in the 20-year period.

Prior to 1973, then, the major source of growth in output and employment in the food industry arose from increased export demand for meat and dairy products. Optimistic projections of the beneficial effects of Common Market membership on increased sales led to greatly increased investment from private and State funds in new enterprises and in plant expansion and modernisation. After EC accession, most of the FEOGA grants to the Irish food industry were concentrated on the meat and dairy sectors. However, events since 1973 have frustrated much of the plans for further growth. A Cooper and Lybrand study sponsored by the Industrial Development ment Authority noted that the fall-off in cattle numbers in 1975 had meant that many new, highly capitalised meat plants were running at less than half capacity. Temporary or permanent plant closures, or firm failures resulted in reduced employment. The IDA consultants recommended a moratorium on further investment aid to the industry until capacity was more fully utilised. In the dairy sector, while total milk supply has grown, the supply available to some of the larger, merged organisations has fallen far below capacity with resultant cost increases and financial distress. The surplus of dairy products throughout the EC has led to the curtailment of FEOGA grants to dairy processors.

A further drawback has been that net output has represented a small proportion of gross output in both the meat and dairy industries, only 13.0 and 14.5 per cent respectively, in 1973, as compared to 21.0 per cent for all food, 69.3 per cent for all drink and 36.2 per cent for all manufacturing. The problem of low value added applies also in the bacon and milling industry. Meat processing is still largely confined to slaughtering and cutting the carcase into sides or quarters. Dairy processing has actually regressed in terms of value added by increasing the proportion of milk converted into butter and skim milk, the products supported by EC intervention. Given the exogenous factors pushing up labour costs, firm survival can only be secured by the adoption of productivity increasing technology or alternatively by reducing numbers employed.

The main reason for the low value added in the Irish food industry is that firms are still using the basic processes of producing butter or fresh beef used in more primitive economies. Much of the ultimate preparation of food for the consumer is done by firms in the UK or elsewhere, so that many Irish processors put little effort into marketing. Ireland remains primarily a producer of commodities in a form not identifiable by consumers. With one or two major exceptions Irish food processors do not market abroad the packaged goods which generate high value added and a high employment content because of the various services they include. However, recognising the need for further processing in Ireland is a far cry from actually achieving the same. The history of past attempts has not been very encouraging, the foreign companies presently carrying out the further processing of Irish commodities will fight to retain their business, and recent structural changes in the Irish food industry may hinder future attempts at further processing in Ireland.

In the past, the Irish food industry's aversion to production and exports of packaged consumer goods has made sense in terms of the structure of Irish firms and the nature of the marketing chain. Most of the firms owed their existence either to local supplies of raw materials (milk, cattle, pigs) or to local market needs for animal feed, flour, baked goods, etc. A few large firms with capabilities for nationwide marketing of packaged goods had emerged before Independence, e.g., Guinness, Jacobs. However, most of the present nationwide marketing organisations have evolved through growth, takeover or merger only in the last twenty years, and in many cases even more recently. In export marketing, most produce of Irish food firms was sold on the UK wholesale provision exchanges. Price was determined by the state of the market on a given day, and the origin of the product was often concealed by further processing. Aided by legislation which gave it monopoly powers over foreign marketing of Irish dairy products, Bord Bainne made the first major and effective move to establish a consumer franchise abroad for Irish dairy products. In the early 1960s, it launched Kerrygold Irish creamery butter on the UK market, succeeding not only in increasing its market share but also in obtaining a premium price.

Bord Bainne was aided by changes that were gaining momentum in the UK food marketing system. The arrival of supermarket chains with their head-on (and successful) attack on resale price maintenance forced the long-established provision chains (Liptons, Sainsbury, etc.) to modernise, and drove most of the viable independent retailers into voluntary groups. The result was a concentration of food purchasing into fewer and larger hands. Chain and group buyers went direct to suppliers when possible, so that the traditional wholesale markets' role dwindled. Processors wooed retail buyers for scarce shelf-space with a proliferation of new brands, convenience features (pre-cooked, pre-packaged, prepared, etc.) and the support of national television and press advertising. As the price of entry rose, there were many mergers among food processors, until in almost every product group the market was dominated by a few firms.

During the 1960s, there were two notable attempts by Irish firms to emulate the success of Bord Bainne. The Pigs and Bacon Commission struggled to establish a brand image for Irish bacon with UK consumers in the face of problems of continuity of supply, variable quality and the difficulty of identification of Irish bacon at point of sale. Erin Foods, a subsidiary of the Irish Sugar Company, attempted to leap ahead of the world food industry in use of a new technology, Accelerated Freeze Drying (AFD). Erin Foods attempted to develop simultaneously new production systems, a new sales force, a varied product range, national distribution in the UK and brand identification with wholesalers, retailers, caterers and consumers. A consultant's report requested by the Irish Government commented that any one aspect of the Erin Foods' programme would have been a major venture. In tackling the entire programme, Erin Foods ran out of raw materials, finance and managerial experience. However, its greatest difficulties were in marketing. In the UK market, it simultaneously took on some of the most powerful and experienced marketers of packaged foods in the world, including Unilever, Heinz and Nestle. Each of these already possessed a worldwide system of raw material procurement and plant location, a large base of profitable products, a widely known brand image from a long-running investment in consumer advertising, a well-organised sales force, a record of successful introduction of new products, and trade goodwill. Although it was a costly lesson, the Erin Foods experience brought home forcibly to Irish agriculture the difficulties involved in shifting from a commodity to a packaged goods orientation. Erin Foods now concentrates on the domestic market and exports both directly and through a small subsidiary, Heinz-Erin, jointly owned with Heinz.

In the 1960s many other Irish food concerns have grown by takeover or merger and attempted to use the commercial television service to establish domestic consumer loyalty in Ireland. However, success in the domestic market has not been as effective a launching pad for export success as marketing theorists might suggest. In their study of concentration in the Irish food industry, Quinn and Smith have shown that a launching pad for export success as marketing theorists might suggest. In their study of concentration in the Irish food industry, Quinn and Smith (1975) have shown that foreign multinationals dominate the domestic canning, confectionery, margarine and miscellaneous food industries; have large stakes in dairying and milling, and a foothold in the bacon and meat industries. This means that expansion of use of Irish agricultural products, decisions to add more value within Ireland, and control of new product development, must be tailored to the multinationals' overall marketing plans. In many cases, the Irish subsidiary is not free to compete on the UK or other major markets and is only free to export where the parent company does not have an affiliated operation. While it is impossible to quantify the present effects of these limitations, it is clear that they have the power to curtail exports of Irish subsidiaries. Within the European Community trading area, it is likely that the Irish plants of multinationals will specialise in a limited number of lines which will be sold throughout the EC and that all other lines will be supplied from the company's other plants. Within the multinational company, such shifts will have the goal of increasing efficiency. However, they will have large effects on imports, exports and employment in the Irish food industry. Some of these effects will be examined in more detail later.

For the meat processing industry the domestic market takes such a small part of industry output that it provides neither a secure sales base nor a testing ground for new products and marketing innovations. Indeed, the meat industry as an exporter of prime beef is only about a decade old. Because of the growth in cattle numbers during most of that decade, the industry's energies were concentrated on securing the needed finance for plant expansion. When the beef market weakened after 1973, the EC intervention system acted as a disincentive for the industry to attempt new product or marketing initiatives. The Cooper and Lybrand study for the IDA estimated that "in 1974 and 1975 40 per cent and 34 per cent, respectively, of the total output of the (meat) packing industry was consigned to intervention stores." The EC has been unwilling to allow the intervention system in Ireland to be altered to take account of the high seasonality of Irish marketings and to avoid the necessity for storage on this scale. Efforts to frame a monopoly export marketing body on the lines of Bord Bainne are favoured by the farming organisations but opposed by many processors. Indeed, it is doubtful if such a marketing monopoly could be successful unless it had control over grading and standardisation of products, assured continuity of supply and a very, very large development and promotional budget. The bacon industry shares similar problems. In its case, however, its strong domestic sales base has acted as a disincentive to impose the necessary discipline and make the necessary long-term commitment to developing larger export sales. Both the Department of Agriculture study team and (more recently) Igoe (1975), have suggested the urgency of major rationalisation of existing plants, but progress has been slow in that direction.

Prior to EC entry, the dairy industry was able to use a large home market as a sales base while its state-appointed monopoly export marketing arm, Bord Bainne, aggressively promoted Irish dairy products throughout the world. It was thought that EC entry would provide almost limitless sales potential relative to foreseeable supplies of Irish dairy products. In the event, market growth has been excellent both in volume and price although some sales of skim milk have been made into intervention stocks. On a community-wide scale, however, intervention stocks of butter and skim milk had reached such proportions by 1976 that the European Commission proposed an action programme to reduce milk deliveries to dairies and a temporary suspension of national and Community aid measures which might encourage the expansion of milk production. It is difficult to see how the past rate of growth of the Irish dairy industry can be maintained under such circumstances unless Ireland can justify some special exemptions from general EC production controls.

Membership of the EC has brought other mixed blessings to the Irish dairy industry.

Since State trading monopolies are not permitted under EC rules, on Ireland's accession Bord Bainne gave up its semi-state body status and became a marketing co-operative with dairy processors as voluntary members. The increased stake of diversified non-Irish firms in the Irish dairy industry, and the growth of some Irish dairy firms to a size where an independent export effort becomes feasible, have begun to challenge Bord Bainne's supremacy over export marketing. In 1977, such a challenge led the Board to accept a programme for marketing cheese from Ireland under a Tortoise brand acceptable to four major cheese producers rather than under the Irish Kerrygold brand. Clearly, these large, diversified producers could market Irish cheese and other dairy products abroad under their own brands and thus jeopardise the accumulated investment in the Kerrygold brand. Some of the implications of this clash for output and employment will be discussed in the next section.

While the EC intervention system for dairy products, has been instrumental in absorbing excess supplies and maintaining prices, it has led the Irish dairy industry to increase its dependence on butter and skim milk. It has led to a reduction in the demand for milk products used by other industries, such as confectionery, baking and miscellaneous food. New product development has been neglected, and exporting has been hindered by the decision to produce dairy products such as yogurt for the Irish market under a foreign licence which limits exports. In the last decade, the industry's energies have been involved in a massive effort to rationalise, consolidate, modernise and absorb new technologies of milk assembly, handling and processing. Bord Bainne was expected to sell what was produced. However, if the reorganised industry is to make further progress it must now devote more of its energies to innovative marketing.

The dairy industry, more than any other Irish food sector, has suffered from seasonal variations in the supply of raw materials. Accordingly, plant, equipment and transportation have all had to be geared to meeting peak summer needs, and are greatly under-utilised in trough periods with resultant increases in average fixed costs. Dairies have sought to use their permanent staff in diversified off-peak activities, although these have been limited by the rural location of most dairies and the seasonal nature of farm activities. The growth of milk production in recent years has resulted in a more pronounced absolute and relative gap between peak and trough supplies. As a result, many creameries have established incentives for winter milk, and much research and advisory effort has gone into systems for earlier calving. No one knows how far off season production can be pushed before the extra cost of incentives, winter feed, etc., outweigh the extra savings from better utilisation of plant and equipment. To date, no dairy organisation has been willing to refuse milk, but this may be the ultimate answer to failure to control future peak supplies. Seasonal supplies in dairying create less acute marketing problems than those in fresh meat where an Autumn glut of supplies has consistently driven prices downwards and forced diversion of large quantities into intervention storage. Efforts to encourage more even production of Irish beef would require an end to the heavy reliance of the Irish cattle industry on Summer grass. It is difficult to see how such a switch can come as long as CAP grain prices move up in step with meat prices, and price incentives for winter feeders remain inadequate. Furthermore, there is no evidence that such a change in CAP or in the intervention system is anywhere near.

The experience of the Irish food industry is not unique in the European Community. EC studies suggest that in the United Kingdom, Belgium and France, growth in the food industry has been slower than in all manufacturing, many firms and plants are small and outdated, and there is overcapacity in most major food sectors. While Belgium and France have experienced some inroads by large multinationals, the United Kingdom food industry is dominated by multinational processors and marketers of packaged food products. Most UK food markets for consumer products are modified oligopolies. The price of entry is a high cost sales and promotion campaign which, if initially successful, must be sustained at a more moderate level over many years. For example, the average expenditure on press and television advertising for butter would be about one per cent of sales, for cheese about two per cent. New entrants would require a much higher percentage initially.

However, the UK and other European markets still have central exchanges, food brokers, contract buyers and other agencies willing to handle traditional Irish commodity exports. Irish exporters, therefore, must weigh the possible benefits from direct access to consumers for identified Irish products, against the higher costs of that marketing approach. The Irish Government, in its concern for the provision of more added value and employment in food processing within Ireland, must examine, if and how, Irish firms could be compensated to encourage them to add more value in Ireland. As will become clear in the next chapter exhortation or monetary grants alone will not be effective encouragement.

Chapter 12

Irish Food Industry – Forces for Change

ONE of the clichés of all commentaries on present-day society is the increasing rapidity of change. However, the cliché is particularly appropriate to the Irish food industry. As well as the usual changes in consumption patterns, production technology and marketing systems, decision makers have had to operate within a new set of institutional constraints as a result of Ireland's accession to the European Community. That Community itself has experienced much turmoil about its future direction so that even the new rules of the game are by no means final. The Irish food industry is, perhaps, more adaptable than some tradition-enshrouded parts of the food industry in France, Belgium and Italy. Our close ties with the United Kingdom have exposed the Irish food industry to many pressures in the past. However, if the spirit of the original European Common Market survives and free movement of labour, capital and goods is allowed to prevail, the shape of the Irish food industry will be vastly altered by 1990 with resultant impact on output and employment.

The Irish market will become vulnerable to food products such as butter, bacon and meat which are directly competitive with traditional Irish products. With advancing incomes, Irish consumers will demand a wider variety of food experiences, continental cheeses, wines, delicatessen foods, etc., in which other EC countries have a long lead in successful production and marketing. In addition, Irish consumers will be tempted by innovative combinations of products and services from multi-national packaged foods producers. In the domestic market, Irish bacon, dairy, canning, confectionery, etc., firms will no longer be competing against each other in a fairly select club, but will be open to the assault of any aggressive European organisation. Accordingly, Irish food businesses will operate with reduced advantages in the Irish market. Some important advantages will, of course, still remain, proximity to Irish markets; some consumer allegiance to products which give employment in Ireland, etc. However, increasingly the survival of Irish firms will depend not on their being Irish but on their being internationally competitive.

The greatest change required by Irish food firms to make them internationally competitive will be in organisation. Organisation in business involves the successful acquisition and deployment of labour and capital to carry on one or more activities at sufficient reward that promoters, managers, employees and capital can be retained in the business. Some of the major tasks which must be simultaneously organised in the food industry are procuring of raw materials, using efficient technology, matching workers to machines, securing finance, marketing existing products and reinvesting some of the surplus earned in replacement technology and products. Advances in computers and telecommunications have made co-ordination and control independent of place so that a multinational operation in Europe can be as easily organised from London or Geneva, Brussels or Dublin, although most businesses prefer to have their headquarters near major financial or political centres. Computers have also facilitated the management of very large and diverse operations, so that frequently, despite a tendency to become bureaucratic and top heavy, large companies can retain the economies of scale gained in production, finance or marketing. In addition, through their size and diversity, multinational concerns can cushion the effects of very large errors in production, new product development, etc. Diversity may take the form of integrating backwards to secure raw material supplies, integrating forward into wholesaling or retailing, horizontal integration of similar production units or conglomeration of unrelated products.

It is the authors' belief that by 1990, multinational companies will dominate most sectors of the European food market. This is not to say that they will be the sole form of organisation, but rather that other forms will only survive if they are compatible with the goals of the multinationals. Thus, many smaller producers of speciality items, suppliers of local or regional needs, brokers, agents and other providers of services to the food trade will continue to flourish. Irish processors can either gear themselves to compete directly with the multinationals as Erin Foods attempted, or settle for a foothold in those parts of the market where more limited forms of organisation can still survive.

Their choice will also be influenced by the changing structure of the food distribution system. While the United Kingdom and West Germany converted most of their retail food business to chain and/or supermarket operation during the 1960s, the other European countries were slow to follow. However, in the early 1970s, supermarkets and hypermarkets (similar in size to US style supermarkets) have made rapid gains in the rest of Europe. The more food products are marketed in processed and standardised form, the narrower becomes the custom for the specialised boulangerie, patisserie, charcuterie, etc., where the skill of the operator is critical. The hypermarket simulates the village shopping street, with all food needs under one roof and one management, but linked in a chain of almost identical hypermarkets. Already in the US and the UK, as the different chains become more alike, the individual boulangerie or café or other speciality is reappering under the hypermarket roof, adding a new twist to the cycle of change. However, for mass marketers in Europe by 1990, the key marketing channel will still be the supermarket or hypermarket chains.

The result of this will be an increase in concentration of purchases by retailers and an increase in direct buying, with further pressure on traditional wholesale, auction and commodity exchange trading. Direct buying will take two main forms, purchase of heavily promoted, branded items from large processors, and purchase of unbranded products to which the retailer can affix his own brand. The processor uses branding to maintain a monopoly over a section of consumers regardless of where they shop. To the processor a stable or growing market share is essential for planning of production, sales and profitability. The retailer is quite happy to handle branded items on which his customers are already presold. However, the retailer also likes own brand merchandise because it attracts customers to his stores, it can be sold profitably at a price below comparable branded items, and it is a useful defence against unwelcome pressures from marketers of branded products. Its usefulness is limited by the fact that most consumers prefer nationally branded items, only a few standardised products can generate sufficient sales to justify the cost of own branding, and processors, from their interest in a narrow range of products, can consistently out-perform retailers in new product development and consumer appeal.

While these advantages of the large processors are also important in the market for food eaten away from home, branding and mass promotion decrease, and price competitiveness increases in importance. Based on experience in the US as *per capita* incomes rise, eating away from home could account for anything up to a third of all food consumption in Europe by 1990. Its growth is related to the increasing number of workers employed by large organisations which provide subsidised mid-day meals, to more working women, increased travel, increased dining out for pleasure, and increased provision of food under various welfare programmes in schools, hospitals, etc. The purchasing and preparation of raw foods, and the cooking and garnishing of dishes can usually be done more cheaply and often more skillfully on a large scale in a food plant than in a catering establishment. In particular, the cost of skilled labour limits individual preparation of meals to expensive restaurants. The high cost of eating out has led in the US to the development of large limited-menu fast food chains, some of which have made inroads into Europe. However, their growth in Europe is likely to be limited by the expansion of food sales in pub, tavern and wine shop outlets already in existence. Capturing a share of the European catering market would require consistent quality and supply and competitive pricing. Given the likely increase in concentration among buyers, breaking into such a market may require considerable ingenuity on the part of new Irish entrants.

Despite the changes foreseen by 1990, a scaled down version of traditional food distribution systems is likely to survive alongside the multinational processors, large caterers and retail chains. Wholesalers will continue to service numerous small retailers and restaurants, brokers to procure fresh produce, fish and other specialised products on behalf of retail chains, and agents to represent large processors and small where the expense of an individual sales force is not warranted. In a diverse and healthy economy there will always be many growing, declining or specialised products which lack the scale, continuity or profitability to fit comfortably into standardised mass marketing programmes. However, the traditional sector will remain vulnerable to attack from the organised financial and market power of the multinationals. It would be extremely risky for the Irish food industry to rely heavily on the traditional sector.

So, in which direction, can, should or will the Irish food industry now organise and what might be the output and employment consequences of that choice? In some cases, the options are already gone. As already pointed out, multinationals dominate the canning, confectionery, margarine and miscellaneous food industries and have large stakes in dairying and milling. Sugar production is in the hands of a single State-sponsored company, which under EC rules no longer has a monopoly of sales on the Irish market. A single Irish public company dominates the Irish biscuit market but is a prime target for absorption by a multinational. Quinn and Smith (1975) report at least a dozen multinationals with interests in the Irish dairy industry. Accordingly, the only major sectors of the Irish food industry which have the option to design an independent organisation are the remaining co-operative and private firms in the bacon, meat and dairy industries. At the time of writing, 1977, the prevailing policy is for each firm to make production decisions independently, leaving a common marketing agency to carry the brunt of export marketing research, development and promotion within the limits of its powers. These powers vary from near monopoly in the case of Bord Bainne to mainly promotional in the case of the Irish Livestock and Meat Board (best known by the initials of the Irish name, CBS, for Coras Beostoic agus Feola), with the Pigs and Bacon Commission occupying an intermediate position.

The present organisational structure of the bacon, beef and dairy industries would be adequate for continuation of commodity style marketing. It could, with minor modifications, handle increased cutting or vacuum packing of beef and bacon. However, the single greatest strength of the Irish food industry is its ability to produce livestock and dairy products in very large quantities. If the maximum output, value added and employment in Ireland were to be derived from this rich natural resource, it should be converted into consumer packaged goods for the export market. Clearly, such an approach would require co-ordination, discipline and control within the Irish food industry comparable to that achieved within the integrated multinational organisations. It could be achieved by single large companies such as Cork Marts – Irish Meat Packers, or by groups of complementary firms in the dairy or meat industries. Given exceptional goodwill and foresight on the part of member firms, it could be achieved by an amalgamation of most or all of the Irish bacon, meat or dairy processing firms. The entire Irish beef industry would just about compare with a minor multinational in terms of sales or employment. For example, Unigate, the UK producer of dairy products, baby foods, etc., in 1973 had over five times as many employees as the entire Irish dairy industry.

Enormous problems would be involved in developing one or a number of powerful processors of packaged consumer goods in the Irish bacon, meat or dairy industries. Since so many of the firms are farmer-owned co-operatives, they have had considerable difficulty in financing both long-term investment and working capital. Yet the necessary finance could probably be acquired more easily and rapidly than the necessary production and marketing expertise in handling consumer products in international markets. Of course, the Irish food industry could choose a less daring path, a continuation of the status quo or some minor excursions into higher value added products. The chief difficulty with such a strategy is that it creates no permanent export demand for identifiably Irish food products. Without a consumer franchise the Irish supplier of commodity foods remains susceptible to price pressures from the wholesalers, processors and retailers on whom he must rely. In turn, it leaves Irish processors vulnerable to takeover by multinationals wishing to secure alternative sources of supply of raw materials.

It is worth considering what the impact on output and employment might be of a general takeover of the Irish food industry by multinationals. On the plus side it would provide the financial, technological and marketing expertise now missing in certain sectors. The multinational production facility in Ireland could be used as a base for expanded exports. On the other hand, the multinationals could equally well opt to use their Irish plants to service only the Irish market or to concentrate on a limited number of lines of production or import supplies for the Irish market from abroad. The British multinationals already operating in Ireland, having regard to the existing overcapacity in much of the UK food industry, have been reluctant to use their Irish plants as an export base. US, Japanese or other multinationals might be more willing to expand output of high value-added products in their Irish plants. And, of course, multinationals are freer to shift out of Ireland, if advantages arise in raw materials, labour, investment incentives, etc., in other countries. Clearly, an Irish food industry dominated by multinationals would only expand if real economic advantages accrued in Ireland compared to those available in competing countries. Finally, multinationals prefer to emphasise brand rather than origin in their promotion, so that the domination of multinationals would not be compatible with a dominant role for Bord Bainne or similar organisations which emphasise the Irish origin of products.

The domination of the Irish food industry by foreign, especially UK, multinationals already far exceeds what other major countries such as Japan and France have considered prudent if they are to retain control of their own country's affairs. Since such a large portion of Ireland's output, exports and employment are at stake, it seems imperative that Irish interests, either public or private, make a stand in the meat, dairy and bacon industries, and attempt to weld together large financial and marketing entities capable of aggressive expansion into other countries. Much export marketing now involves the exporting of entire plants, technology, supporting capital as well as Irish-produced raw materials and packaged consumer goods. Without Irish-based multinationals, the Irish food industry will not be able to compete on these fronts with the Danes, Dutch, New Zealanders, etc. It is by no means certain that Irish Government policy could reverse the present course of development of the Irish food industry. Before any large new State-sponsored or private Irish-based multinational was set up, intensive studies would be required to determine feasibility and possible effectiveness. Ultimately, an Irish-based multinational will be subject to the same disciplines of competitive cost of raw materials, comparable efficiency of technology, competitive pricing of its products and skilled marketing as every other food processor. Control of food firms will only make a contribution to the Irish GNP or employment, if it is accompanied by competitiveness on these other fronts.

Chapter 13

The Irish Food Industry in 1990

THE first major constraint on the growth of the food industry to 1990 is the availability of domestic raw materials. In a previous section, we suggested that gross agricultural output could grow by 38.8–45.6 per cent between 1975–90. However, we did not indicate what that would mean in terms of output of leading products. We suggested that the economic forces favouring livestock production would mean a fairly constant acreage devoted to crops with growth in feeding barley acreage compensating for declines in other cereals and fodder crops.

Using the crop acreage projected for 1990 in Table 7.4 and estimates of trend yield and average 1973–75 prices developed by Murphy *et al.* (1977), we can expect an increase in gross output of crop products of 16.5 per cent by 1990 (Table 13.1). Only feeding barley output is likely to grow faster than average. In the absence of evidence to the contrary, we assumed constant output in poultry, and output increases in sheep and lambs and pigs consistent with market growth projected in Table 10.1. Accordingly, the potential growth in cattle and dairy products compatible with the overall growth of GAO would be about 50 per cent. A number of hypothetical combinations of cow numbers, yield increases and cattle output could generate this level of increase. However, particularly in cow numbers, past trends can be misleading because of the influence of non-recurring factors. For example, in the 1960–75 period, total cow numbers rose from 1,283.7 thousand to a peak of 2,151.3 thousand in 1974, an increase of 67.6 per cent. However, increases or improvements in agricultural land and declines in tillage and horse and sheep numbers facilitated a 26 per cent growth, so that the increase in cow numbers due to increased intensity of production was 41.6 per cent. Assuming that the same increase in intensity could be achieved in the 1975–90 period would indicate that Irish agriculture could support 3,046.2 thousand cows in 1990. Using the ratio of cattle output to cow numbers reported by Baker *et al.* (1973), (.89), suggests that level of cow numbers could sustain an annual output of 2,711 thousand cattle, only 17.4 per cent above the most recent peak in 1975. It should be noted that an increase in cow numbers by 1990 of almost 900,000 would require an additional 4.5 million tons of barley equivalent, much of which would have to be imported.

Projecting milk output is even more hazardous, involving, as it does, assumptions about the proportion of dairy cows, yield per cow, and the proportion of production classified as output. The EC action programme for milk contains incentives for switches from dairy cow to beef cow production. Accordingly, one might expect the

Table 13.1: *Estimated agricultural output 1975 reported and 1990 projected*

Product	Unit of quantity	Estimated quantity		Estimated value		Unit price	Per cent change 1975–90
		1975	1990	1975	1990		
Horses	(1000)	14	14	5,147	5,147	367.65	—
Cattle and Calves	,,	2361	2771	370,370	434,687	156.87	+17.4
Sheep and Lambs	,,	1852	2638	28,262	40,256	15.26	+42.4
Pigs	,,	1534	2471	52,908	85,225	34.49	+61.1
Poultry	,,	22523	22523	16,038	16,038	—	—
Total Livestock	Value	—	—	472,725	581,353	—	+23.0
Milk – consumer	1000 gal.	138	150	36,633	39,819	265.46	+8.7
– industrial	,,	624	1482	154,939	367,981	248.30	+137.5
– other	,,	5	5	717	717	143.40	—
Other Livestock Prod.	Value	—	—	19,490	19,490	—	—
Total Livestock Prod.	,,	—	—	211,779	428,007	—	+113.2
Total Livestock and Livestock Products	,,	—	—	684,504	1,009,360	—	+47.5
Wheat	1000 tonnes	189	137	10,737	7,783	56.81	-27.5
Oats	,,	28	23	1,258	1,033	44.93	-17.9
Malting Barley	,,	230	259	12,811	14,426	58.40	+12.6
Feeding Barley	,,	447	864	22,082	42,682	49.40	+93.3
Sugar Beet	,,	1430	1283	18,132	16,535	12.68	-10.3
Potatoes	,,	408	407	15,630	15,592	38.31	-0.2
Other Crops	Value	—	—	24,938	24,938	—	—
Total Crops	Value	—	—	105,588	122,989	—	+16.5
Turf	1000 ton	1084	1084	7,967	7,967	7.35	—

proportion of beef cows to total cows to increase somewhat. We have assumed that the proportion would increase from 32 per cent in 1975 to 36 per cent in 1990. We have used the method suggested by Murphy *et al.* to estimate yield and output of milk. Milk output in 1990 is estimated to be more than double and milk yields 52 per cent higher than in 1975. The amount consumed as whole milk is likely to be little above 1975 levels, so that the milk available for industrial use would rise by 137.5 per cent. To absorb such an increase, the dairy products' manufacturing industry would have to achieve a growth rate comparable to that achieved in the 1960–75 period when export markets expanded dramatically. Our demand estimates in previous sections suggest that Irish beef output by 1990 can be readily absorbed by domestic and Community markets, but that only about one-quarter of the additional output of dairy products can be so absorbed at constant 1975 price levels. Thus, dairy marketers face the formidable task of either developing new markets within an already self-sufficient EC or of finding large new outlets throughout the world.

Not surprisingly, then, the second major constraint on growth in the food industry is the final demand for its output. In the case of beef, mutton and lamb and dairy products, we have already shown the vital importance of growing export markets. If the present imbalance in dairy product markets continues, production of livestock and livestock products may be altered in a number of ways, either by a reduction in total cattle numbers as the dairy herd contracts, or in a greater than expected swing to beef herds. Accordingly, the supply of raw materials envisaged in Table 13.1 can be taken as the upper limit of production in 1990 in the bacon, meat and dairy industries. In the meat industry, we have assumed a continuation of live exports of 500,000 cattle and a doubling of 1973 slaughterings for domestic consumption, leaving 1,817 thousand cattle for slaughter, 2.8 times the number handled by meat packers in 1973. However, a number of other sectors of the food industry import much of their raw materials so that output and employment is heavily dependent on demand factors. The few demand analyses of major food products available give either conflicting results or projections far outside the range of past experience. Accordingly, in the canning, confectionery, baking, margarine and miscellaneous food industries, and in distilling and mineral waters, we have assumed that volume of output increases at the same annual average rate as in the 1953–73 period. Sugar industry demand in the past has come from the consumer market and from the dairy, confectionery, baking and mineral water industries. Expansion in industrial demand is likely to offset any decline in household consumption. However, since it is impossible to predict how much the Irish sugar industry will be hit by inroads from UK importers, we have assumed 1990 volume constant at 1973 levels. The milling industry contains two components with contrasting trends, the flour industry and the animal feedstuffs industry. Applying the same weights to each sector in 1990 as used by the CIP in 1973 and assuming the same annual average rate of change as in the 1953–73 period suggests a 50.6 per cent increase in demand for the milling industry by 1990. This would be compatible with the increase in livestock numbers already envisaged, a decline in flour milling and a higher proportion of compound feeding stuffs fed by Irish farmers. Future prospects for the brewing and related malting industry are clouded by the uncertainties of export markets and Government taxation programmes. Assuming some decline in exports, the growth of the industry can probably be contained within the level indicated for malting barley production in 1990. Together, brewing and malting absorbed 162,000 tons of malting barley in 1973. Projected availability in 1990 would exceed that level by 59.9 per cent. Such a growth rate would be similar to that actually achieved by the brewing industry and below that achieved by the malting industry in the 1953–73 period.

The volume index for 1990 estimated as described above was multiplied by the cost of raw materials, fuel and packing materials in 1973, to give an estimate of the cost of materials in 1990. The ratio of net output to gross output in 1990 was estimated by projecting the trend values for 1953–73 where such a trend existed, or using the mean value where no trend existed. For example, the ratio of net output for the dairy industry in 1990 was estimated to be 18.5 per cent, the cost of materials at 1973 prices £472,501,500. The value of gross output in 1990 at 1973 prices equals £472,501,500 ÷ (1 – .185) = £579,756,000 (Table 13.2).

The most notable feature of the estimates for both value of gross output and net output is the expected doubling in size of the overall food and drink industries by 1990 (Table 13.2). However, these industries, bacon, meat and dairy, would account for 81.3 per cent of the increase in gross output and 65.4 per cent of the increase in value of net output in the food sector, while in the drink sector, the brewing and soft drink industries would account for 88.5 per cent of the growth in gross output and 91.5 per cent of the increase in value of net output. In dairy and soft drinks, there must be grave doubts about whether markets can actually grow at the indicated rates. In all industries the much faster growth of net output than employment would permit very substantial (on average about 70 per cent) increases in net output per person employed over the 18-year period.

Given the prospect of large increases in the volume and value of gross and net output in the Irish food industry, the number of persons employed in 1990 will be largely dependent on the rate of increase of labour productivity. As already pointed out, productivity increases have been a feature of all sectors of Irish manufacturing both food and non-food. Under the pressures of competition likely to be faced between now and 1990, it seems reasonable to expect that labour productivity in the food industry will have to increase at least at the rate achieved in the 1953–73 period. It is impossible to predict in which sectors new production and marketing technologies will emerge most rapidly. One might assume that labour productivity would grow at the same rate in all sectors. However, we have previously suggested that some products are much more amenable to the introduction of mechanical handling, automation, continuous processes, etc., than others. Accordingly, we have assumed that labour productivity grows in each sector at the actual rate experienced in that sector in the 1953–73 period.

Table 13.2: *Value of gross and net output and persons employed in the Irish food industry, 1973 and 1990 projected*

	Industry	Value of gross output (£'000) at 1973 prices		Value of net output at 1973 prices		Persons employed (number)	
		1973	1990	1973	1990	1973	1990
1.	Bacon	84,605	136,284	16,189	37,887	4,600	6,365
2.	Meat	149,066	423,845	19,373	60,186	4,240	8,124
3.	Dairy	232,822	579,756	33,874	107,255	7,710	10,828
4.	Canning	22,587	51,270	9,030	24,919	3,360	5,278
5.	Milling	93,150	153,226	19,691	42,597	4,710	4,656
6.	Sugar	24,165	26,998	7,966	10,799	1,895	1,262
7.	Confectionery	27,596	32,036	11,370	14,448	4,880	3,280
8.	Baking	48,845	54,738	23,550	27,369	9,245	8,184
9.	Margarine	6,275	11,140	2,305	5,570	445	608
10.	Miscellaneous	13,741	62,143	4,513	24,733	1,700	5,198
	Total food	702,852	1,531,436	147,864	335,761	42,785	53,783
11.	Distilling	4,493	9,466	2,094	5,111	340	145
12.	Malting	7,715	13,326	2,298	4,664	360	133
13.	Brewing	51,390	87,034	40,504	69,627	4,535	4,753
14.	Soft drink	17,918	63,990	11,627	40,890	2,290	2,870
	Total drink	81,516	173,816	56,523	120,292	7,525	7,902
	Total food and drink	784,368	1,705,252	204,384	476,053	50,310	61,685

Source: Gross and net output from CIP 1973.

$$\text{Gross output } \frac{1990}{1973}$$

$$\text{Persons employed 1990} = \frac{\text{Gross output } \frac{1990}{1973}}{\text{Labour productivity } \frac{1990}{1973}} \times \text{persons employed 1973}$$

While the resulting estimates suggest an increase in persons employed in the food and drink industry in 1990 of 11,375 (22.6 per cent), the increases are again heavily concentrated in a few industries. The most extreme case is the miscellaneous food sector which is a "catch-all" category for many different types of food processing. It showed an actual decrease in labour productivity in the 1953–73 period. On the assumption that its labour productivity to 1990 would increase at the food industry average, it would require three times as many workers in 1990 as in 1973. The meat industry would require an increase of almost 4,000 persons over 1973, the dairy industry almost 3,000, the canning and bacon industries about 2,000. Absolute declines in employment would be expected in half of the food and half of the drink sectors. Just as in gross and net output growth, the dairy and meat sectors' performance would be critical to any absolute growth in employment in the food sector.

It is possible to check how realistic these employment projections are against the estimates prepared by Murphy et al. (1977). They used time series equations to relate employment in administrative (including clerical and supervisory) and industrial categories to the volume of raw materials used in the main products produced (for example, in the dairy industry, cheese and other manufactured milk). By means of a survey of processors they obtained estimates of the direct and indirect employment content of each product, and of expected productivity increases in the next decade. They then estimated employment needs at given levels of raw material supply and selected mixes of products with differing labour requirements. Higher intensity of labour use would tend to occur in conjunction with a higher ratio of net output (and value added) to gross output.

Our estimate of employment in the meat industry for the given supply of cattle would imply a labour intensity higher than that of Murphy's et al. high intensity estimate for 1985, but one certainly achievable by 1990. Our estimate of employment in the dairy industry is lower than that suggested by Murphy et al. for a comparable level of milk input at each level of intensity specified. Clearly, our results would suggest a greater reliance on low labour intensity products such as butter and skim milk powder than that assumed in Murphy's et al. medium or high intensity options. Any differences between our projections and those of Murphy et al. can be explained by differences in the mix of labour intensive products. Clearly, even very substantial increases in production in the Irish food industry in 1990 will not generate increased employment unless there is a fairly widespread swing to higher value added and/or more labour intensive products.

In summary, growth in output of Irish agriculture to 1990 is likely to arise from yield increases of crops on a constant acreage and from increased concentration on cattle and milk production. Supplies of milk and beef for processing will more than double. In addition, the miscellaneous food and soft drink industries are likely to grow very rapidly. As a result, despite slow growth in a number of food sectors, total gross and net output of the Irish food and drink industry can double between 1973 and 1990. However, even at the trend rate of increase in productivity, total employment will only rise by 22.6 per cent, with trends in the meat and dairy industries being most critical to overall growth in employment.

SECTION IV

POLICY IMPLICATIONS

Chapter 14

Implications of Output and Employment Projections to 1990

THE projections for growth of agriculture and related food and drink processing have important national and regional implications. For example, the decline in the number of farmers and farmworkers by 1990 may range from 70 to 100 thousand depending on relative farm-non-farm incomes in the intervening years (see Walsh and NESC discussion of Walsh's projections). We would lean towards the lower end of this range. The projected increase of 11,375 jobs in food and drink processing will fail totally to compensate for that decline. Baker and Ross's (1975) study suggests that an increase in non-agricultural autonomous employment of that magnitude could lead to an increase in induced employment of two-thirds of that amount, say 7,583 jobs, so that the total increase in non-agricultural employment could reach 18,958. Clearly, growth in food processing of the magnitude envisaged will provide additional jobs but will contribute less than 5 per cent of the total new jobs needed by 1990.

It is also possible to make some estimates of the impact of agriculture and the food industry on the national accounts by 1990. Income arising in agriculture has tended to rise less rapidly than gross output as Irish farmers have moved to more input-intensive production systems. Thus, for a 38.8 per cent increase in real gross output in the 1975–90 period, we might expect income arising in agriculture to increase at two-thirds of that rate (say 25.7 per cent). Thus, income arising in agriculture might rise from £524.0 million to £659 million at 1975 prices, an increase of £135 million. Such an increase in agricultural income would be multiplied through the economy. Henry suggests that the average income multiplier as the result of a unit change in expenditure on output of agricultural livestock was about 1.264 in 1968. Applying that multiplier to the additional income arising in agriculture suggests a total impact on net national product of £171 million.

Wages and salaries accounted for 46.5 per cent of net output in the food industry and 30.6 per cent of net output in the drink industry in 1973. Although there has been a secular tendency for these ratios to decline, they can be used as an estimate of the upper limit of wages and salaries. Using the estimates of 1990 value of net output from Table 13.2, wages and salaries should rise from £86.1 million to £192.9 million in 1990 at 1973 prices, an increase of £106.8 million. Assuming that wages and salaries rise at the same rate in the induced sector, the total rise in wages and salaries attributable to increased food and drink processing would be of the order of £178.0 million (i.e., one and two-third x £106.8 million). Other national product at factor cost including profits, interest, dividends, rent, etc., averages close to one-third of wages and salaries, so that the total addition of the food industry and related sectors to net national product in 1990 would be £237 million at 1973 prices or £332 million at 1975 prices.

Accordingly, we might expect that the extent of growth envisaged for farming and food and drink processing would generate increased net national product by 1990 of £503 million (equivalent to 17 per cent of 1975 NNP). While its impact on employment would not be large, the contribution of the agriculture and food industry would be just sufficient to maintain NNP per head at the 1975 level in 1990 at expected rates of population growth.

However, because so much of its increased output would have to be sold abroad, growth in agriculture and the food industry would have a major impact on the balance of payments. Of the additional gross output of 38.8 per cent possible by 1990, 13.4 per cent could be absorbed in the domestic market leaving 25.4 per cent additional output to be sold abroad. At 1975 prices this would amount to £231.4 million at the farm level. However, the net increase in the balance of payments could be reduced by two factors, the increased imports of inputs needed to generate the additional output, and possible declines in the real price of dairy products if supply potential continues to exceed demand. Imports of live animals, feeding stuffs, fertiliser, insecticides, petroleum products, and agricultural machinery, tractors, trucks, etc., amounted to £123.9 million in 1975. If the ratio of such imports to gross agricultural output remained the same in 1990 (which would require increased imports of feeds to be offset by declines in other agricultural imports) increased exports of agricultural products would be offset by increases of £31.5 million in related imports. It is not possible to predict what the drop in real price of dairy products might be or how it would reflect on milk price to the farmer. To some extent, price declines could be offset by increased value-added content of exports. Accordingly, £200 million (at 1975 prices) seems a reasonable estimate of the maximum net improvement in Ireland's balance of payments which could result from the projected increases in agricultural output. This is compatible with that estimated by Murphy et al. in their trend model for 1985. It is not possible to distinguish the multiplier effect of improved export earnings from that already estimated from income arising in agriculture, but some separate impact would occur.

The impact of growth in agriculture and in the food industry will not be felt equally in all regions. The decline in numbers of farmers and farmworkers will be most severe in the western half of the country and may be quite moderate in the better lands in Leinster and Munster. Output is also likely to grow most rapidly on these better lands so that the bulk of any increase in food industry employment is likely to be concentrated where the number of farmworkers has fallen least. Thus the net employment effect will be least favourable in the west. In turn the multiplier effect of increased employment or earnings will be weakest in the west. Accordingly, the regions which are already disadvantaged because of lack of vigour in their agriculture and food processing industries are likely to become even more disadvantaged by 1990. For these regions, the development of non-agricultural based industries will remain very important.

We should point out, too, that the smaller the region in which an economic stimulus is received, the larger the leakages and the smaller the multiplier effect will be. For example, much of the benefit of an increase in demand for a rural food processor will be leaked away in increased demand to out-of-town hauliers, agents, etc., increased salaries and wages to out-of-town residents, increased purchases of out-of-town goods by resident employees, etc. The actual multiplier effect will have to be estimated for each region or locality individually. The Lough Egish food city complex represents one effort to increase internal linkages in a rural food processing environment. However, such linkages within nearby Irish food industries are still rare. Induced employment and earnings in many rural areas will grow less rapidly as a result of agricultural and food industry growth than the national average.

Certain other social consequences may follow from the growth of agriculture and the food industry. Farming itself is likely to continue to provide predominantly male employment. The food industry and drink industry have also tended to be male dominated. Seventy-two per cent of wage-earners in the food and 100 per cent in the drink industry in 1968 were males. Of salaried workers, 66.3 per cent in the food and 63.3 per cent in the drink industry were male. Only in the canning and confectionery industry were more than half of wage-earners female. The gradual mechanisation and automation of processes requiring physical strength, the slow increase in the proportion of salaried employees, and legal and social pressures for equal opportunity for female employees and married women, may lead to a gradual increase in the proportion of females employed. However, changes are likely to come slowly, so that by 1990 probably two-thirds of all food and drink industry employees will still be male. So, while the net impact of the food and drink industry on local economies may be smaller than might appear from aggregate figures, these sectors will remain as key providers of off-farm employment for males in rural areas.

Chapter 15

Conclusions

THIS survey of output and employment potential in the Irish food industry has ranged over many topics and drawn upon evidence from many sources. In this chapter we attempt to summarise the main findings and their implications for future policy initiatives.

We began with the premise that Ireland needs 30,000 new jobs each year to 1990, and set out to examine how many of these could be provided by an expanded food industry. We documented the land, labour and market constraints under which Irish farmers have operated in the past. On the assumption that market incentives would continue to favour livestock enterprises, we estimated that Irish agriculture could increase output by 38.8–45.6 per cent (or about 2.2–2.5 per cent per annum) between 1975 and 1990, primarily in beef cattle and dairy products, an estimate considerably below most other official and unofficial projections.

Next we looked at market potential for Irish agricultural products. Assuming constant real prices at 1975 levels and continued economic growth at the rates achieved in 1960–70, we estimated that sales within the EC could absorb an added 21.3 per cent of Irish agricultural output over and above 1975 levels by 1990. Almost half of this increase would be absorbed in territorial Ireland, while Great Britain would continue to be the second largest outlet for Irish agricultural products. Accordingly, at constant prices, Irish agriculture would have large excess productive capacity, especially in dairy products. Given the fact that there was likely to be a Community-wide surplus of dairy products, we suggested that continuation of the present intervention system was neither feasible nor economically desirable. It appeared to us that if prices over time were allowed to approximate more nearly to free market levels, Irish producers of dairy products would be likely to increase their share of the EC market and would be in a better position to exploit emerging third country markets.

We then examined the output and employment effects in the food industry in 1990, of achievement of the projected levels of output in agriculture. Under quite optimistic assumptions about growth in final demand and in value added per unit of output, we found that while gross and net output might double, trend increases in labour productivity would mean only an additional 11,375 jobs. This increase, plus a possible 7,583 induced jobs in other sectors, would be swamped by the prospective job losses in agriculture, about 10,000 male and female each, and about 50,000 other agricultural workers. Successful exploitation of the availability of home produced raw materials for the meat and dairy industries would be vital to achieving even modest employment growth in the food industry.

The achievement of a 2.2 per cent annual rate of growth in agricultural output and successful processing and marketing of that output would have other beneficial effects on the Irish economy. Income arising in agriculture could, by 1990, be sustained at a level about 25 per cent above the record level achieved in 1975. Multiplier effects in the processing and related sectors would generate additional net national product by 1990 equivalent to 17 per cent of 1975 NNP. Since population is expected to grow at about that rate in the 1975–90 period, growth in agriculture and food would be just sufficient to maintain *per capita* NNP if all other sectors of the economy remained constant. In addition, successful export marketing of the increased output of agriculture and processing could produce a net addition of £200 million to the nation's balance of payments. While it is not possible to say what the impact of growth will be on different regions, it is clear that the food and drink industry will remain a major source of income and a key provider of male employment in rural areas.

In the course of this study, we have highlighted many of the problems which act as a constraint on faster growth of output and employment in the Irish food industry. In reviewing these here, it is not our intention simply to repeat an already familiar litany of woes but to suggest in each case what step our analysis suggests might be taken to reduce the constraints to growth. We should indicate, initially, however, that we do not see any single golden rule or new political or economic alignment which can, on its own, give the guaranteed growth which Governments seek. If rates of growth in output or employment higher than we have projected are to be attained it will be as the result of small gains on many fronts. Given the generally inelastic demand for agricultural products, increased output without increased markets will lead to lower returns, and increased markets require that the necessary adaptations in processing, packaging, etc., have been made. Even small gains in any of these areas, however, may require very large changes in attitudes, modes of operation and investment. Only the participants themselves can decide whether the game is worth the candle.

Taking into account both supply and demand factors, it is our view that the growth of Irish agriculture should be concentrated on cattle and dairy products. There are a number of areas, for example, the south-east, where soil, climatic and scale factors make tillage a viable proposition. Likewise, in some poorer hill or mountain soil, sheep can yield a consistently higher return than cattle. A small number of producers have the managerial and technical skill to produce pig and poultrymeat profitably, especially for the home market. However, we would suggest that for the mass of Irish farmers a gradual build-up of the livestock-carrying capacity of their land is the most solid basis for sustained growth.

Since cattle production is so dependent on land availability, much attention needs to be directed to the physical and environmental limitations of Irish land for grass production, and to structural problems such as size of farm, fragmentation of holdings, inability or unwillingness of landholders to utilise their holdings and other factors which reduce livestock-carrying capacity. While estimates are available as to what increases in grassland productivity could be achieved under experimental conditions of control and management, more applicable estimates are needed of the productivity increases that are possible on different kinds of farms with the present level of management. In addition, estimates are needed of the initial investment costs, operating costs and potential earnings from alternative methods of increasing grassland productivity. MacCanna has shown that development farmers frequently lack either own resources or borrowed funds needed to move to a higher plane of productivity. Too often in the past, growth targets have not been related realistically to the existing farmers and their resources. There may be some argument for setting future growth targets at a local level based on the assessment by farmers, advisers, researchers, bankers and others of all relevant local conditions.

The conventional approach to increasing the productivity of Irish grassland involves the use of additional inputs, primarily fertilisers, but also weed-killers, herbicides, veterinary preparations, hormonal injections, etc. However, these costs recur against each acre or each livestock unit. In the case of dairy cows, where the added returns in terms of increased milk yield at a stable price can be captured quickly, Irish farmers have been willing to invest in the needed inputs. However, in the cattle industry, farmers have been unwilling to commit themselves to recurring costs when selling price can vary widely, and can rapidly negative any gains in productivity. It would seem that emphasis might be more fruitfully devoted to means of increasing productivity which are either low-cost or non-recurring, or those which use the operator's time or managerial skill rather than purchased inputs. Included are land drainage, improved rotation, more efficient utilisation of existing grazing, improved timing of fertilisation (rather than increased amounts), and better timing of mowing, silage-making, silage-treatment, etc. The agriculturalist's emphasis on more output at any cost so long as it is a "modern" technique, must be replaced by the economic emphasis on likely added returns from added cost. Ultimately, of course, the ideal farm operation would be able to balance the use of both low-cost and high-cost techniques of increasing productivity against possible returns, but in the meantime we must make the best possible use of farms as they actually are.

Some of the structural problems of Irish farming are being lessened by the passage of time. The proportion of land being farmed by younger farmers is increasing, and the number of older farmers is diminishing. Even more rapid transfers of land would certainly boost productivity further. While there is almost certain to be further tinkering with inducements for older farmers to retire and leave their land, it appears that certain benefits of holding land for speculation, as a hedge against inflation, or for status in the community, have not been well understood or adequately taken into account in setting inducements. Similar problems have arisen with regard to part-time farmers. Conway suggests that part-time farmers tend to reduce the intensity of their operations and produce lower net output per acre than comparable full-time farmers. However, the part-time farmer is making a rational allocation of his time to achieve a desired level of income from both farm and non-farm activities. In many cases, off-farm work is as a wage-earner in a factory, subject to one or two weeks' notice of dismissal. The farm is not only a source of supplementary income but also an insurance policy against unemployment, as well as being a hedge against inflation and a speculative investment as in the case of the full-time farmer. Persuading the older full-time farmer to give up his farm is an easier task because it is merely hastening what he knows to be inevitable. As well as improved inducements, there needs to be experimentation with transfer systems such as the New Zealand share-milking arrangements which make a gradual transition possible for both new and retiring farmers. However, as experience in many other countries has shown, there is a strong tendency for more (rather than less) farmers to go part-time. Clearly, if the full potential of land operated by part-time farmers is to be tapped, Ireland needs to develop research and advisory programmes specifically geared to the limitations of part-time farmers. For example, they may benefit very much from group ownership or operation of farm machinery and equipment.

One final comment needs to be made about structural change in Irish agriculture. While selective programmes may attempt to encourage older farmers to retire or younger farmers to enter farming or expand their enterprises, the higher the general price support systems are under CAP, the more reluctant will existing marginal farmers be to leave farming. Two main planks of CAP are in a sense bidding against each other, one encouraging the other discouraging structural change. We need to know much more about the processes by which different categories of farmer decide on entry to or exit from farming if we are to avoid the waste and frustration resulting from conflicting policies.

However, our study suggests that structural problems are not likely to be the major constraint on the growth of Irish agriculture in the period 1975–90. Rather, it will be the availability of markets for the modest annual growth in output that can be achieved. CAP has up to this point shown a tendency to encourage growth in production throughout Europe at a rate faster than consumption has grown, so that surpluses have become a feature of EC food markets. Since surpluses are rightly regarded as an indicator of excess resources devoted to production, and further resources must be used to store or dispose of these surpluses, there will be pressure to keep surpluses within a historical relationship to annual consumption. Accordingly, increased production for sale to intervention is likely to be discouraged, as is presently the case with respect to milk. Ireland will be handicapped by its dependence on dairy markets which have most consistently tended towards surpluses, but will benefit by the likely continued growth in beef markets. It will also be handicapped by the expected sluggish growth in the UK, its main external market. Lastly, at the present level of CAP support prices, we would argue that trade is inhibited in the main products of interest to Ireland. Ireland faces the difficult task of increasing its sales by increasing its share of a stable or slowly growing market and appears to lack any clear-cut edge in competitiveness which would make such an increase in market share likely.

The only way out of such an impasse is the general lowering of the real price and freeing of intra-EC trade in agricultural products under CAP, a task which has begun with the help of inflation in 1976 and 1977. Initially, this would have two unpleasant effects for Irish agriculture. Incomes would fall for a time and the number of marginal operators going out of business would increase. However, the available evidence suggests that attrition would be most severe on the highly intensive farms in the UK and the Netherlands, and on the least efficient producers in all countries. To some extent, part-time farming and farming to an advanced age would be discouraged. The core of full-time, commercial farmers in Ireland should be little affected since, as owner-occupiers, with little hired labour, borrowed capital or purchased inputs, most of the residual reward to land, labour or capital accrues directly to the farmer.

The reduction in price accompanied by free trade and the ending of intervention buying on a large scale would have fairly rapid beneficial effects for Ireland. Given its comparative advantage in the production of beef and dairy products, Ireland should be able to expand its market share not only in the UK but also in West Germany and other major EC markets. Furthermore, the general reduction in price should stimulate both final demand for raw products such as milk and beef, and intermediate demand for their use in dairy-based products, prepared meals, restaurant dishes, etc. Ireland would be able to develop export marketing programmes for its agricultural products based on the permanent features of consumer demand rather than on the shifting sands of politically administered regulations.

A reduction in CAP prices would also make it feasible for Irish producers to diversify production into those forms of product most desired by the market. A start might be made in this direction by granting cheese prices the benefit of intervention support as is currently now permitted in Italy. Lower CAP prices would also permit Irish exporters once again to actively seek out third country markets where demand for all forms of meat and dairy products may be growing more rapidly than in the Community itself.

How far would CAP prices have to fall before EC food markets would come into equilibrium? The answer would vary for each commodity depending on the position and slope of the supply and demand curves and on the access permitted for third-country suppliers. Much more empirical evidence would be needed to provide a definitive answer. However, we would suggest that overall price reductions would be modest when resulting shifts in the position and movements along the supply and demand curves were taken into account. In particular, the ending of producer expectations of rising prices or assured markets would be a major disincentive to production.

Inevitably, the reduction of CAP price supports would reduce incomes for some farmers. This is as it should be. Those who cannot compete should be discouraged from farming. From a welfare point of view, it may be desirable to support their incomes during the transitional period. However, those income supports must be so geared that they hasten and ease the transition out of farming, not ease the process of staying in farming.

If these steps to adjust CAP are taken, Ireland can hope to sell at a profit all the output it can produce by 1990. In addition, the food and drink processing industry is more likely to expand if it has a plentiful supply of raw materials at a lower price. However, it too, must overcome a number of obstacles to expansion involving its raw material supplies, processes, organisation and co-ordination.

There is a real danger of unbalanced growth in the supply of milk and beef in the 1975–90 period. Basically, beef output grows at the same rate as the number of cows, but milk output (through increasing yields) grows faster. While it would appear that all the additional beef can be profitably sold, marketing the available industrial milk will only be possible if CAP is radically altered or some unforeseen stimulus to demand emerges. The balances can be redressed to some extent by greater incentives for conversion of dairy herds to beef production or by increasing the output of beef per cow. The latter technological change would involve economic and social ramifications in Irish agriculture which are little understood at this time. As things now stand, any forced cutback in dairy cow numbers causes a proportionate reduction in cattle available for the beef processing factories. In like vein, we have argued that the availability of other inputs to the Irish food processing industry, especially pigs, sheep and lambs, and fruits and vegetables are dependent on the relative profitability of cattle and contract tillage crops such as sugar. There is, therefore, no reason to anticipate any rapid change in the product mix of Irish farmers.

Accordingly, the brunt of expanded output and employment in the Irish food and drink industry must be borne by the meat, dairy and miscellaneous foods and soft drink industries. The soft drink industry is geared predominantly to the home market and is already dominated by multinational brands so that its growth is largely outside the scope of Irish agricultural policy. The miscellaneous food group is a "catch-all" category of which fishery products account for about one-half and potato crisps for one-quarter. However, miscellaneous foods include many of the new forms of preparation, processing, packaging, etc., which meet the demand for a wider variety of food experiences as consumers' incomes rise. It is an area where encouragement by the Industrial Development Authority could induce multinational concerns to establish export-oriented new ventures in Ireland.

The bacon, meat and dairy industries have an opportunity to expand under Irish control. To do this, they must become organised on a scale and at a level of efficiency comparable to the multinational food giants against whom they must compete or to whom they must sell in export markets. They must be comparable in terms of financial resources, technological advancement, research and development, and marketing and promotional expertise. The dairy industry comes closest to this goal at present as production units have merged into larger groupings and responsibility for export promotion has been vested in Bord Bainne. However, it is the authors' opinion that such a set up is vulnerable to undermining from within by the UK multinationals which already have subsidiaries in Ireland. Bord Bainne's leadership role can be weakened. The present structure of the meat industry, while largely geared to exploitation of existing channels of distribution, could expand the sale of vacuum packed beef. However, it could not support a general industry move into higher value-added products to meet the developing needs of the working housewife, the catering industry, fast food chains, etc. The big gains in value added are to be found, not in shifting from butter to cheese or from fresh to vacuum-packed beef quarters, but in providing the many services now associated with food consumption. The Irish meat industry has suffered temporary setbacks in developing the concentrations of resources needed to launch itself into the 1980s. However, the process of concentration needs to be continued if it is to remain under Irish control.

The alternative is the extension of multinational control to all the Irish food and drink industry. This result would not necessarily be adverse for the Irish economy. If raw material resources, labour productivity or other key factors favoured continuing or expanding operations in Ireland, multinationals would do so. However, they would not have the same commitment, as, for example, Bord Bainne, to utilising Irish agricultural output through the good and the lean years.

The food and drink industry can make an important contribution to income and employment in the Irish rural community. However, alone it can only meet a fraction of the additional jobs needed as a result of the continuing numbers leaving agriculture and the rising number of unemployed school-leavers. The contribution it can make may be diminished unless the Irish Government and industry leaders can persuade our EC partners to make the changes in CAP necessary to stimulate community-wide demand rather than production.

REFERENCES

BAKER, T. J. and M. ROSS, 1975. *Employment Relationships in Irish Counties*, Dublin: The Economic and Social Research Institute, Paper No. 81.

BORD BAINNE, *Annual Report*, Dublin: Bord Bainne.

BORD BAINNE, *Five Year Marketing Plan*, 1977–81, Dublin: Bord Bainne.

CONFEDERATION OF IRISH INDUSTRIES, 1977, "Food Processing in Ireland: Achievements and Prospects", Dublin: Food, Drink and Tobacco Federation.

CONWAY, A. G., 1975. "Inter-farm Differences in Growth of Output", *Economics and Rural Welfare Research Report*, Dublin: An Foras Talúntais, pp. 36–39.

COPELAND, J. R., and E. W. HENRY, 1975, *Irish Input-Output Multipliers*, 1964 *and* 1968, Dublin: Economic and Social Research Institute, Paper No. 82, August.

CROTTY, R., 1966. *Irish Agricultural Production*. Cork: Cork University Press.

FENNELL, ROSEMARY, 1973. "The Common Agricultural Policy: A Synthesis of Opinion", *Centre for European Studies*, Wye College.

FRAWLEY, J., J. M. BOHLEN and T. BREATHNACH, 1975. "Personal and Social Factors Related to Farming Performance in Ireland", *Irish Journal of Agricultural Economics and Rural Sociology*, 5: 157–181.

FRAWLEY, J., J. M. BOHLEN and T. BREATHNACH, 1975, "The Relationship of Scale and Farm Management Performance in Ireland", *Irish Journal of Agricultural Economics and Rural Sociology*, 5: 145–55.

GARDINER, M. J., and P. RYAN, 1969, "A New Generalised Soil Map of Ireland and its Land-Use Interpretation", *Irish Journal of Agricultural Research* 8: 95–109.

GRIFFITH-JONES, W., 1977, "Adding Value to Agriculture Output", Paper presented to *Agricultural Graduates Business Association Annual Conference*, Dublin.

HAFERKAMP, WILLIAM, 1976. "Lack of Fresh Political Impulses", *Intereconomics*, November, pp. 296–298.

HANNAN, DAMIAN, 1972. "Kinship, Neighbourhood and Social Change in Irish Rural Communities", *Economic and Social Review*, Vol. 3, No. 2.

HEAVEY, J. F., and B. C. HICKEY, "Farm Management Survey, 1966–69, three-year report", Dublin: *An Foras Talúntais*.

HICKEY, B. C., 1970. "Economies of size in Irish Farming", *Irish Journal of Agricultural Economics and Rural Sociology*, Vol. 3, No. 1, pp. 45–60.

HICKEY, B. C., 1975, "Developments in the Structure and Level of Regional Agricultural Production", Paper presented at Conference on *Rural Development in a Regional Context*, Dublin: 20th November.

HICKEY, B. C., and J. CONNOLLY, 1975. "Economics of Feeding Concentrates to Overwintering Beef Cattle", *Economics and Rural Welfare, Research Report* 1975, pp. 24–26, Dublin: An Foras Talúntais.

HICKEY, B. C. and B. KEARNEY. 1976. "Prospects and Problems of Growth in Irish Agriculture", Paper presented at conference on *Agricultural Development, Prospects and Possibilities*, Dublin.

HORAN, CON, 1976. *New Zealand, a Look at New Zealand Agriculture, Especially the Dairying Industry.* Report on a visit to New Zealand, October 1975.

IGOE, M., 1975. "The Structure of the Irish Pig Processing Industry", *Irish Journal of Agricultural Economics and Rural Sociology* 5: 109–129.

INDUSTRIAL DEVELOPMENT AUTHORITY, 1977. *Development Study of the Irish Beef Packing and Processing Industries,* prepared by Cooper and Lybrand Associates, Ltd., Dublin.

JOHNSON, ROGER G., and A. G. CONWAY, 1976. "Factors Associated with Growth in Farm Output", Paper presented at Agricultural Economics Society of Ireland Meeting, 16th June, p. 51.

JOSLING, T. E. and D. I. F. LUCEY, 1972, "The Market for Agricultural Goods in an Enlarged European Community", Proceedings, *Agricultural Economics Society of Ireland,* Vol. 4, No. 1, pp. 22–28.

KARG, G., and H. LAUENSTEIN. 1976. "An Econometric Model of the Beef and Pork Market of the Federal Republic of Germany", *European Review of Agricultural Economics,* 3:4, pp. 523–548.

KEANE, M., 1975. "The Food Industry and Rural Development" at Conference on *Rural Development in a Regional Context,* Dublin: 20th November.

KEARNEY, B., 1974, "Change and Adjustment in Irish Agricultural Production", Paper Presented at Conference on *Current Adjustments in the Rural Economy,* Dublin: 26th November.

KEARNEY, B., 1976. "Outlook for Irish Agriculture", paper presented to *Agricultural Science Association,* November.

KELLEHER, C. and P. O'HARA, 1976. "Adjustment Problems of Farmers in the Context of Agricultural Development", Paper presented at Conference on *Agricultural Development Prospects and Possibilities,* Dublin.

KENNEDY, KIERAN A., 1971. *Productivity and Industrial Growth, The Irish Experience,* Oxford: Clarendon Press.

LEE, J., 1975. "An Analysis of Land Potential for Grazing in Ireland with Particular Reference to Farm Size Relationships", *Journal of the Statistical and Social Inquiry Society of Ireland,* Vol. 23, Part I, pp. 149–182.

LEE, J. and S. DIAMOND, 1972. *Soil Survey Bulletin No. 26,* Dublin: An Foras Talúntais.

LEE, J. and L. J. O'CONNOR, 1976. "Sugar-beet Yields in Ireland with Special Reference to Spatial Patterns", *Irish Journal Agricultural Research* 15: pp. 25–37.

MacCANNA, PEADAR, 1976. "The Development of Irish Agriculture", Presidential address to the Agricultural Economics Society of Ireland, Dublin: 13th October.

McCARRICK, R. B., 1966. Proceedings Tenth International Grassland Congress, Helsinki.

McFARQUHAR, A. M. M., 1971. *Europe's Future Food and Agriculture,* Amsterdam: North-Holland Publishing Co.

MAYES, DAVID G., 1975. "The Changing Price of Butter", *European Review of Agricultural Economics* 2 (3), pp. 339–359.

146

MITTER, SWASTI, 1975. "Problems of Estimating Demand Parameters in a Complete System of Equations: An Analysis of the Demand for Food Items in the U.K.", *European Review of Agricultural Economics*, Vol. 2, No. 3, pp. 307–338.

MURPHY, JOHN A., 1976. *A Comparative study of Output, Value-Added and Growth in Irish and Dutch Agriculture*. Dublin: NESC Report No. 24, Stationery Office.

MURPHY, J. A., J. O'CONNELL and S. J. SHEEHY, 1977. *Alternative Rates of Growth in Irish Agriculture*, Dublin: NESC Report No. 34, Stationery Office.

O'CONNELL, JOHN J., 1977. "Measurement and Growth of the Food Production and Distribution Industry in Ireland", read before the *Statistical and Social Inquiry Society of Ireland*, 12th May.

O'CONNOR, R., 1972. "Projections of Irish Cattle and Milk Output Under EEC Conditions", *Economic and Social Review*, Vol. 3, No. 3, pp. 455–473.

O'RIORDAN, W. K., 1976. "The Demand for Food in Ireland 1947–73", *Economic and Social Review*, July, pp. 401–415.

O'ROURKE, A. D., (forthcoming), "Aggregate Demand for Animal Feed in Ireland", *Irish Journal of Agricultural Economics and Rural Sociology*.

O'ROURKE, A. D., 1977. "Management Entry into Irish Agriculture", unpublished, Dublin: Economic and Social Research Institute.

O'ROURKE, A. D. and T. McSTAY, 1978. "The Demand for Fertiliser in Ireland", *Irish Journal of Agricultural Economics and Rural Sociology*.

OSKAM, A. J. and B. WIERENGA, 1975. "Marketing of Butter in the EEC. Demand Functions and Policy Alternatives, with a Restriction to Four Member Countries", *European Review of Agricultural Economics*, Vol. 2, No. 2, pp. 193–234.

QUINN, G. and L. F. SMITH, 1975. *A Study of the Evolution of Concentration in the Irish Food Industry*, 1968–73, Brussels: Commission of the European Communities.

RYAN, M., 1974. "Grassland Productivity, 1. Nitrogen and Soil Effects on Yield of Herbage", *Irish Journal of Agricultural Research* 13: pp. 275–291.

RYAN, M. and T. FINN, 1976. "Grassland Productivity 3. Effect of Phosphorus on the Yield of Herbage at 26 Sites", *Irish Journal of Agricultural Research* 15: pp. 11–23.

SCULLY, JOHN J., 1971. *Agriculture in the West of Ireland, A Study of the Low Farm Income Problem*, Dublin: The Stationery Office, September.

TOLLEY, G. S., 1970. "Management Entry into U.S. Agriculture", *American Journal of Agricultural Economics*, 52: (4) pp. 485–93, November.

VERMEER, J., 1975. "Effects of Trade Liberalisation on U.S. Agriculture", *Agricultural Economic Research*, Washington, D.C.

WALSH, T., 1964. "The Role of Fertilisers in Increasing Agricultural Production in Ireland", Symposium on Agriculture, Cracow, Poland.

WEBER, ADOLF and ERNST WEBER, 1975. "The Structure of World Protein Consumption and Future Nitrogen Requirements", *European Review of Agricultural Economics*, Vol. 2, No. 2, pp. 169–192.

WEINSCHENCK, GUNTHER, 1973. "Issues of Future Agricultural Policy in the European Common Market", *European Review of Agricultural Economics*, Vol. 1, No. 1, pp. 21–46.

BIBLIOGRAPHY

A. *Official Publications:*
  (i) *Irish:*
(All published in Dublin by the Stationery Office).
  Central Statistics Office, 1976, Census of Industrial Production – Principal Results for 1973, Irish Statistical Bulletin, June 1976.
  Central Statistics Office, Census of Industrial Production Analysis of Principal Results, 1968 (ISB) December 1970; Analysis of Principal Results, 1963 (ISB) September 1965; Analysis of the CIP, 1968 supplied to ISB, March 1973; Analysis of the CIP 1963 supplied to ISB March 1968.
  Central Statistics Office, Census of Population, 1961.
  Central Statistics Office, Census of Population, 1971.
  Central Statistics Office, 1976, Household Budget Survey, 1973, Vol. 1, summary results.
  Central Statistics Office, Irish Statistical Bulletin.
  Central Statistics Office, National Farm Survey: Interim Report 1955–56, I(IJ and) SB September 1956; Second Interim Report 1955–56, I(IJ and)SB, March 1957. First Interim Report, 1956–57, I(IJ and)SB, September 1957. Second Interim Report 1956–57, I(IJ and)SB, December 1957; Interim Report 1957–58, I(IJ and)SB, September 1958; Financial Results for farms included throughout the years, 1955, 1956, 1957, 1958, December 1959.
  Central Statistics Office, The Trend of Employment and Unemployment.
  Central Statistics Office, Trade Statistics of Ireland.
  Department of Agriculture, 1963, Report of the survey team on the Bacon and Pigmeat industry.
  Department of Agriculture, 1963, Report of the survey team on the Beef, Mutton and Lamb industry.
  Department of Agriculture, 1963, Report of the survey team on the Dairy Products Industry.
  Department of Agriculture and Fisheries, 1970, Report of the Committee on the Review of State Expenditure in Relation to Agriculture.
  Minister for Agriculture and Fisheries, Annual report of.
  National Economic and Social Council 1975; Population and Employment Projections 1971–86, Report No. 5, contains a study by Brendan M. Walsh called by the same name, February.
  National Prices Commission, 1973. The Animal Feedstuffs Industry in Ireland, Occasional Paper No. 11, December.
  National Prices Commission, The Egg Industry in Ireland, Occasional Paper No. 17, September.
  National Prices Commission, 1974, The Irish Flour Industry, Occasional Paper No. 16, May.
  Programme for Economic Expansion, November 1958.
  Second Programme for Economic Expansion, 1964.
  Third Programme for Economic and Social Development, 1969.

  (ii) *Other:*
  Commission of the European Communities, 1975, A study of the evolution of concentration in the food industry for the United Kingdom, Vol. 1, Brussels, October.
  Commission of the European Communities, 1975, Étude sur l'evolution de la concentration dans l'industrie alimentaire en Belgique, Brussels, September.

Commission of the European Communities, 1975, Étude sur l'evolution de la concentration dans l'industrie alimentaire en France, Brussels, October.

Commission of the European Communities, 1976. Restoring balance on the milk market, Action programme, 1977–80. Bulletin of the European Communities, Supplement, 10/76.

Commission of the European Communities, Yearbook of Agricultural Statistics (annual). Statistical Office of the European Communities, Luxembourg.

Northern Ireland, Digest of Statistics, (annual), HMSO, Belfast.

OECD, Agricultural Projections for 1975 and 1985, OECD, Paris.

OECD, Food Consumption Statistics, 1955–1973, OECD, Paris.

OECD, Study of trends in world supply and demand for major agricultural commodities, OECD, Paris.

UK Central Statistics Office, Annual Abstract of Statistics, HMSO, London.

UK Ministry of Agriculture, Fisheries and Food. EEC Agricultural and Food Statistics, 1972–75, HMSO, London.

United Nations: Statistical Yearbook (annual), UN, New York.

United Nations, Production Yearbook (annual), UN, New York.

United Nations, The Population Debate: Dimensions and Perspectives. Papers of the World Population Conference, Bucharest 1974, Vol. 1, New York.

UN Economic Commission for Europe, 1977, European market for meat and livestock, 1975 and 1976. UN, ECE, Geneva.

UN, FAO, Agricultural Commodities – Projections for 1975 and 1985, Vols. I and II, UN, FAO, Rome.

UN, FAO, Commodity Review and Outlook (annual), UN, FAO, Rome.

UN, FAO, 1974, Review of meat production and demand projections to 1980, UN, FAO, Rome.

US Department of Agriculture, "The Impact of Dairy Imports on the U.S. Dairy Industry", USDA–ERS, Agricultural Economic Report No. 278, January.

B. *Books and Articles:*

ATTWOOD, E. A., 1972, "The Structure of Irish Agriculture and its Future Development", Proceedings of the Agricultural Economics Society of Ireland, Vol. IV, No. 1, Dublin.

BAKER, T. J., R. O'CONNOR and R. DUNNE, 1973, "A Study of the Irish Cattle and Beef Industries", Dublin: The Economic and Social Research Institute, Paper No. 72, July.

BLAGDEN, P. and M. RYAN, 1972, "Potassium in Irish Farming", Proceedings of the Fertiliser Association of Ireland.

THE ECONOMIC AND SOCIAL RESEARCH INSTITUTE

Broadsheet Series:

1. *Dental Services in Ireland*   P. R. Kaim-Caudle
2. *We Can Stop Rising Prices*   M. P. Fogarty
3. *Pharmaceutical Services in Ireland*   P. R. Kaim-Caudle
                    assisted by Annette O'Toole and Kathleen O'Donoghue
4. *Ophthalmic Services in Ireland*   P. R. Kaim-Caudle
                    assisted by Kathleen O'Donoghue and Annette O'Toole
5. *Irish Pensions Schemes, 1969*   P. R. Kaim-Caudle and J. G. Byrne
                                                             assisted by Annette O'Toole
6. *The Social Science Percentage Nuisance*   R. C. Geary
7. *Poverty in Ireland: Research Priorities*   Brendan M. Walsh
8. *Irish Entrepreneurs Speak for Themselves*   M. P. Fogarty
9. *Marital Desertion in Dublin: an exploratory study*   Kathleen O'Higgins
10. *Equalization of Opportunity in Ireland: Statistical Aspects*
                                           R. C. Geary and F. S. Ó Muircheartaigh
11. *Public Social Expenditure in Ireland*   Finola Kennedy
12. *Problems in Economic Planning and Policy Formation in Ireland, 1958–1974*
                                                                        Desmond Norton
13. *Crisis in the Cattle Industry*   R. O'Connor and P. Keogh
14. *A Study of Schemes for the Relief of Unemployment in Ireland*
                                                        R. C. Geary and M. Dempsey
        with Appendix   E. Costa
15. *Dublin Simon Community, 1971-1976: An Exploration*   Ian Hart
16. *Aspects of the Swedish Economy and their Relevance to Ireland*   R. O'Connor,
                                                        E. O'Malley and A. Foley

General Research Series:

1. *The Ownership of Personal Property in Ireland*   Edward Nevin
2. *Short-Term Economic Forecasting and its Application in Ireland*   Alfred Kuehn
3. *The Irish Tariff and The E.E.C.: A Factual Survey*   Edward Nevin
4. *Demand Relationships for Ireland*   C. E. V. Leser
5. *Local Government Finance in Ireland: A Preliminary Survey*   David Walker
6. *Prospects of the Irish Economy in 1962*   Alfred Kuehn
7. *The Irish Woollen and Worsted Industry, 1946–59: A Study in Statistical Method*
                                                                        R. C. Geary
8. *The Allocation of Public Funds for Social Development*   David Walker
9. *The Irish Price Level: A Comparative Study*   Edward Nevin
10. *Inland Transport in Ireland: A Factual Survey*   D. J. Reynolds
11. *Public Debt and Economic Development*   Edward Nevin
12. *Wages in Ireland, 1946–62*   Edward Nevin
13. *Road Transport: The Problems and Prospects in Ireland*   D. J. Reynolds
14. *Imports and Economic Growth in Ireland, 1947–61*   C. E. V. Leser
15. *The Irish Economy in 1962 and 1963*   C. E. V. Leser
16. *Irish County Incomes in 1960*   E. A. Attwood and R. C. Geary
17. *The Capital Stock of Irish Industry*   Edward Nevin
18. *Local Government Finance and County Incomes*   David Walker
19. *Industrial Relations in Ireland: The Background*   David O'Mahony
20. *Social Security in Ireland and Western Europe*   P. R. Kaim-Caudle
21. *The Irish Economy in 1963 and 1964*   C. E. V. Leser

General Research Series—*continued*